"Chris Nye has written a lucid, wise l ... W9-DCW-622 life and the hope of the gospel. His expose of American pathology is searing and specific: 'more,' growth, individualism, isolation, pressure, and wealth, to name some of our lethal addictions. His articulation of a gospel alternative is profoundly compelling. Nye invites us to 'take Jesus at his word' concerning dying with him and being raised to life with him. Such trust would entail nothing less than to 'follow him out of America and into the kingdom of God.' Attention must be paid!"

Walter Brueggemann, Columbia Theological Seminary

"This is one of those rare books that can honestly change your life. Fish don't know they are swimming in water, and we don't usually know what air we are breathing either, because it feels so normal. But in this book Chris brilliantly and poetically shows the enormous blind spots of our culture and our lives while gently taking us back to the One who can give us the true and abundant life we are all looking for—Jesus."

Jefferson Bethke, *New York Times* bestselling author of *Jesus > Religion* and *It's not What You Think*

"Could there be a relationship between the loneliness that grips so many lives today and the desire to have 'more'? In this book, which draws on wisdom honed by ministry, Nye helps us see that just is the case. This is a sobering but much-needed book."

Stanley Hauerwas, Gilbert T. Rowe Professor Emeritus of Divinity and Law, Duke University

"This is a calm book but also an incendiary one; it asks questions that you might rather avoid. But it also provides—or at least hints at —solutions to our deep modern dilemmas. I found it strangely settling in this strangely unsettling time."

Bill McKibben, author of *Falter: Has the Human Game Begun to Play Itself Out?*

"We've been drip-fed the lie, especially in the American church, that our private resources and personal influence should be growing if we're doing things right. Chris Nye masterfully exposes this lie in *Less of More*. Much like John the Baptist, Nye is a voice in our wilderness of wealth and waste, brazenly pointing the way to true human flourishing: Jesus must become greater. We must become less. Period. I pray you not only read this book but reorient your life around its message."

Evan Wickham, lead pastor, Park Hill Church in San Diego, CA

"Most of the people I serve are perishing from having too much while so many of our sisters and brothers perish from having too little. Pastor Chris Nye shows us the way to untangle ourselves from being caught in our stuff. Chris' book has some fresh things to say about an age-old human dilemma. You'll find this book to be a great resource in thinking like Christians in a world where God's abundance is enough."

> Will Willimon, professor of the Practice of Christian Ministry, Duke Divinity School, and United Methodist bishop, retired

"The first word most babies speak is *more*. That is the fallen, broken, narcissistic human story. Sadly, *more* is often one of the last words out of our mouth before we die. *More* is our way, our American way. *Enough* is not even a framework we entertain. Nye offers us a new way forward, but not a way of progress that gives us more of what we want. Rather, it gives us what we need. Contentment. The power and the joy of saying that we don't actually need any more than we already have. We are already rich in Christ."

> Dr. A. J. Swoboda, pastor, author of *Subversive Sabbath*, and teacher in Portland, Oregon

"I reserve the word *brilliant* for the rare writer who genuinely brings light to their subject—that gleam of both truth and beauty. Chris Nye earns it. *Less of More* is a winsome strike against our culture's deep sickness: the runaway consumption that devours our humanity as surely as it deflowers creation and degrades our neighbors. Harsh, honest, yet stridently hopeful, *Less of More* will disturb you in the best of ways—toward a change of heart that could change our world."

> Paul J. Pastor, author of *The Face of the Deep: Exploring the Mysterious Person of the Holy Spirit* and *The Listening Day: Meditations on the Way*

"Chris Nye has done us an enormous favor in writing *Less of More*. He contrasts the American story of *more* (growth-isolation-fame-power-wealth) with the biblical counter-narrative (pace-community-obscurity-vulnerability-generosity). It is not another 'get off the rat race' book but a biblical theology of mission with the personal insights that help us live that mission. It troubled me as I saw many of my own assumptions while calling me to follow Jesus deeply."

> Gerry Breshears, PhD, professor of theology, Western Seminary

Less of More

Less of More

PURSUING SPIRITUAL ABUNDANCE
IN A WORLD OF NEVER ENOUGH

Chris Nye

BakerBooks
a division of Baker Publishing Group
Grand Rapids, Michigan

© 2019 by Christopher Nye

Published by Baker Books
a division of Baker Publishing Group
PO Box 6287, Grand Rapids, MI 49516-6287
www.bakerbooks.com

Printed in the United States of America

All rights reserved. No part of this publication may be reproduced, stored in a retrieval system, or transmitted in any form or by any means—for example, electronic, photocopy, recording—without the prior written permission of the publisher. The only exception is brief quotations in printed reviews.

Library of Congress Cataloging-in-Publication Data
Names: Nye, Chris, 1987– author.
Title: Less of more : pursuing spiritual abundance in a world of never enough / Chris Nye.
Description: Grand Rapids : Baker Publishing Group, 2019. | Includes bibliographical references.
Identifiers: LCCN 2018045150 | ISBN 9780801093890 (pbk.)
Subjects: LCSH: Simplicity—Religious aspects—Christianity. | Wealth—Religious aspects—Christianity.
Classification: LCC BV4647.S48 N94 2019 | DDC 241/.68—dc23
LC record available at https://lccn.loc.gov/2018045150

Unless otherwise noted, Scripture quotations are from The Holy Bible, English Standard Version® (ESV®), copyright © 2001 by Crossway, a publishing ministry of Good News Publishers. Used by permission. All rights reserved. ESV Text Edition: 2016

Scripture quotations labeled HCSB are from the Holman Christian Standard Bible®, copyright © 1999, 2000, 2002, 2003, 2009 by Holman Bible Publishers. Used by permission. Holman Christian Standard Bible®, Holman CSB®, and HCSB® are federally registered trademarks of Holman Bible Publishers.

Scripture quotations labeled NIV are from the Holy Bible, New International Version®. NIV®. Copyright © 1973, 1978, 1984, 2011 by Biblica, Inc.™ Used by permission of Zondervan. All rights reserved worldwide. www.zondervan.com. The "NIV" and "New International Version" are trademarks registered in the United States Patent and Trademark Office by Biblica, Inc.™

Scripture quotations labeled NLT are from the Holy Bible, New Living Translation, copyright © 1996, 2004, 2007, 2013, 2015 by Tyndale House Foundation. Used by permission of Tyndale House Publishers, Inc., Carol Stream, Illinois 60188. All rights reserved.

19 20 21 22 23 24 25   7 6 5 4 3 2 1

In keeping with biblical principles of creation stewardship, Baker Publishing Group advocates the responsible use of our natural resources. As a member of the Green Press Initiative, our company uses recycled paper when possible. The text paper of this book is composed in part of post-consumer waste.

To my grandparents,
Gary and Norma Poppinga

Contents

We can stand anything God and nature can throw at us save only plenty. If I wanted to destroy a nation, I would give it too much, and I would have it on its knees, miserable, greedy, sick.

JOHN STEINBECK, to Adlai Stevenson

PART 1

You Probably Thought There Would Be More

Infinite, Unlimited, and Other Lies

At the bottom of the American soul was always a dark suspense.

D. H. LAWRENCE, "The Spirit of Place"

This is a book about how we can obtain a lot of things and still lose everything. It's about how we can expand businesses, flourish economically, advance politically, win converts, change schools, grow churches, and still not have the things we ultimately desire to possess. It's about how social justice can be disappointing, how making money can feel empty, and how a "packed house" can leave the soul vacant. It's about how our economy has grown, but so have our suicide rates. This is a book about people coming to admire you while you lose respect for yourself, and about

how a nation can hold the world in the palm of its hand
while losing the grip on its soul. It's also about escalators.
And drugs. And taquerias. And college. And Britney Spears.
And there's also some consideration given to bees.

But let's first talk about the pope.

Jorge Mario Bergoglio, or Pope Francis as he is called now,
published a little book titled *Laudato Si'*, which literally means
"Praise be to you" in medieval central Italian. The title does
not help much in understanding its central subject. Thankfully,
as is the case for most books, the subtitle is more clarifying: *On
Care for Our Common Home*. Yes, the leader of the world's
largest church wrote a book about caring for the environment.

Laudato Si' is surprisingly theological and thoroughly
prophetic. Reviewing it for the *New York Review of Books*,
climate expert Bill McKibben praised Francis's book, saying,
"*Laudato Si'* stands as one of the most influential documents
of recent times. . . . It turns out to be nothing less than a
sweeping, radical, and highly persuasive critique of how we
inhabit this planet—an ecological critique, yes, but also a
moral, social, economic, and spiritual commentary."[1]

He's right.

And yet: What does the earth have to do with theology?
Why talk about our "spirituality" when talking about gla-
ciers? And why is a pope, of all people, writing about what
we do with our trees? I can hear the Twitter eggs now: *Stick
to the church, Francis.*

But many who have read *Laudato Si'* would tell you what
I will: Francis's argument is incredibly convincing. You leave
that book understanding the *spiritual* weight of the deci-

---

1. McKibben, "The Pope and the Planet."

sions we usually deem "economic" or "political" or "environmental." These issues have more gravitas than our usual categories tell us. Pope Francis brings together data, policy, Scripture, and practical wisdom to convince readers we're not just losing the earth, we're losing ourselves.

"A certain way of understanding human life and activity has gone awry, to the serious detriment of the world around us," Francis argues. "There is a tendency to believe that every increase in power means 'an increase of "progress" itself,' . . . as if reality, goodness and truth automatically flow from technological and economic power as such."[2]

After reading *Laudato Si'*, several questions came to my mind: Just because we advance in technological and economic power, are we really "progressing" as a society? Should there come a time when businesses should just *stop growing*? Or governments should *stop building*? And militaries *stop arming*? Are we going to keep growing larger just for the sake of growing larger? Does bigger always mean better? Is growth always a good thing?

The pope writes about how human beings and material objects like clothes, phones, and computers no longer hold hands nicely. Due to international labor abuses and consumer expectations of cheap clothing, these material relationships have "become confrontational." And in the twenty-first century, it is now "easy to accept the idea of infinite or unlimited growth, which proves so attractive to economists, financiers and experts in technology. It is based on the lie that there is an infinite supply of the earth's goods, and this leads to the planet being squeezed dry beyond every limit."[3]

2. Francis, *Laudato Si'*, §§101, 105.
3. Francis, *Laudato Si'*, §106.

Infinite or unlimited growth.

Does this sound familiar? Surely you could recognize this phrase in the rhetoric of our CEOs and politicians, but haven't you also heard something like this in church? Or maybe even a university or your workplace? Hasn't Facebook or LinkedIn suggested you "expand your network"?

My wife and I live in the Silicon Valley, eight miles from Stanford University. In 2016, Stanford's endowment was $22 billion. No, that's not a typo. Stanford has the fourth-largest endowment in the United States and stands as one of the most influential and affluent universities in the world. Twenty-two *billion* dollars.[4]

In a 2016 episode of his podcast, *Revisionist History*, Malcolm Gladwell interviewed Stanford's then-president, John Hennessy, regarding this outrageous number and, in a polite way, asked him if there would ever be a time Stanford would just call it good and *not* accept any donations. After all, they're quite literally sitting on billions of dollars in assets and investments. "How much is enough?" Gladwell asks.

"How much is enough?" Hennessy repeats. He fumbles for a bit, and then continues: "If our ambitions don't grow, then I think you do reach a point where you do have enough money. . . . I would hope, then . . . that our ambitions do grow." Gladwell presses Hennessy over and over with bizarre possibilities: Would you accept a $10 billion gift? Would there ever be a time where you would tell a massive donor that their money would be better used in the public college system, which educates two hundred thousand students in the state of California compared to Stanford's sixteen

4. Stanford University, "2016 Results."

thousand students? Hennessy doesn't really answer, but ends up settling on a kind of "no." Gladwell translates: "In other words, there really isn't such a thing as too much money at an institution like Stanford."[5]

As Pope Francis put it: "*Infinite and unlimited growth.*" This is what we think we know: if we had more, we could be better, do more; if we could get more money, we could do more good. Yuval Noah Harari, in his landmark book *Homo Deus: A Brief History of Tomorrow*, puts it more flatly and accurately: "From its belief in the supreme value of growth, capitalism deduces its number one commandment: thou shalt invest thy profits in increasing growth. . . . We will never reach a moment when capitalism says: 'That's it. Enough growth. We can now take it easy.'"[6] Capitalism is

5. Gladwell, "My Little Hundred Million."
6. Harari, *Homo Deus*, 245. Harari believes that we have made what he calls "the Modern Covenant," which "offers us power, on condition that we renounce our belief in a great cosmic plan that gives meaning to life" (245). We have taken this deal in order to service our greed and love for unlimited economic growth. Our latest and greatest religion is essentially a growing, capitalistic society. He's right. This deal "demands that we loosen family bonds, encourage people to live away from their parents, and import carers from the other side of the world" (245). His book goes on to suggest that through this deal, human beings have basically "snuck in" meaning alongside capitalism by inventing humanism, Harari's great hope for the next century or two. He unfortunately neglects the nuances of the religious underpinnings of beliefs that he thinks, apparently, came out of thin air. He cleanly divides the world into unfortunately brash binaries when it serves his arguments. This is only one reason to not fully trust him (the other reason is his daft neglect of the Oxford comma). I would love for him to consider how the history of thought is much more tied together than he presents, and that Christian theology and philosophy—along with those of Islam and Judaism, for that matter—should be and must be credited with much of what he tosses up to "science" or "humanism" or, most laughably, "progress." He would do well to read the work of Marilynne Robinson, Luc Ferry, and Terry Eagleton. Still, all Christian leaders—especially pastors in the Silicon Valley—should read Harari's work, as it will help us understand where modern thought is going and should push us to develop a more serious Christian anthropology, something that is much needed. He is, in the end, a gift.

wonderful when it serves us, but somewhere along the line, we began to serve it, and the fallout has been enormous. Our economic model is now our guide for life; it has become our liturgy, our creed: we firmly believe that if we just had more students, or a larger congregation, or a bigger budget, or a larger staff, or more power, we could accomplish so much more. Many of our decisions come from this heresy.

I suppose this book desires to ask two questions in light of this belief: First, is this true? And second, if it is true, what does that say about us? We can put these questions another way: Is it accurate to believe we could *do* more if we *had* more? And does this belief—that real, abundant life comes from the accumulation, or faster growth, of people, resources, money, and power—actually reveal a kind of emptiness in our churches, businesses, nations, families, and schools instead of a fullness? If we work to gain the world, can we also get our soul included in the deal? Or, as we continue to accumulate more and more, do we completely lose it?

I'm sure the last conference you went to included a list of speakers who sold more books, led bigger organizations, had more connections and friends, and had a larger social media platform than most of the people who were *not* on the stage. They're also probably better looking than the average mug. This is because we believe people like that are "successful." But is there nothing for us to learn from those in the audience who have failed? Can we not learn from the guy who ran his church into the ground or the woman who runs a small business with her family? Or what about wisdom from just . . . normal people? Is the wisdom of a poor, single mom beneficial to business leaders? Does the pastor of the small, rural church know *less* about God's kingdom than the megachurch pastor with a CrossFit ministry? Does the teacher who burned out not have anything valuable to say to the teacher who still enjoys helping kindergarten students put on their jackets before recess?

The American Story and the Counter-Narrative

I'm writing this book in order to craft a counter-narrative—a new story—for Christians in the twenty-first century. In order to do that, I will trace the story as it is told now, which I will call "The American Story of More," but alongside that story, I will offer the counter-narrative of how we should live according to Scripture. As clearly as possible, here are the two stories:

The American Story of More
growth → isolation → fame → power → wealth

The Biblical Counter-Narrative
pace → community → obscurity → vulnerability → generosity

The American story begins with the worship of growth: we believe that very few things get worse as they get bigger. As things have grown in our country, however, we have not become more of a community, but less of one. We have become "hyper-individualists" within our churches and economies as they have ballooned.[7] The more we grow, the more we isolate ourselves. Isolation has led to an "Every man for himself" mantra, and with the help of social media, every

7. McKibben, *Deep Economy*, 96.

person is a brand and a product. We're all celebrities now, or so we think. We desire to be known and celebrated for the things we've accomplished. And from there, the route of the hyper-individualist, who is isolated and self-celebrated, is toward a twofold goal: power and money. We want it all, and we want to have made it alone.

The Bible offers something else, a counter-narrative for faithful people under which we can live. It begins with pace, which is often called "humility." Pace and humility mean we live within our means and capacities. As we do this, we realize we actually cannot "do it alone," that "Every man for himself" is a lie. We adhere to a community and are responsible for one another because we understand our limits. When we live in a community, there are no celebrities; rather, we all live in beautiful obscurity. The story is not about a single individual but about a collective family. In maintaining such a community, power seeking and money grabbing are deadly. Instead, the biblical counter-narrative community is one of vulnerability and generosity. We don't grab power; we lay it down. We do not cling to our money; we share it freely because our foundation is built on a man who had it all and freely laid it all down.

The Common Denominator of a Great Life

When you were a child, you wanted great things. You desired to be someone or do something, with very little understanding of the disciplines or natural skill involved in such pursuits. You dribbled a basketball in your yard after watching Michael Jordan. You danced in your room after you saw a Madonna video. You practiced speeches in front of your mirror and wrote songs when no one was home. You stared at screens, videos, and pictures of the kinds of people you desired to become. You had grand ideas about your life once. And then you went to high school.

One difference between a child and an adult is the realization of limits. As Dirty Harry said at the end of his highly unrealistic and surprisingly poetic address to the man he was about to kill, "A man's got to know his limitations."[8] In many ways, this is what growing up is like and why it sucks. We can't all be powerful, famous, and rich. And we apparently need to be OK with it.

But can we all be happy? Can all of us live a kind of life that is satisfactory and full? And is this life dependent on our childhood dreams of what a good life really is? Put another way: Is it possible to never accomplish anything we set out to do, or be less of a parent/student/person than we desired originally, and still be satisfied with our life? Is the abundant, full life possible when scarcity has been a predominant factor in our life? Is there a way to be rich without having much money? Is there a way to be powerful and influential without any authority or a prestigious job title? Can you lead a large organization with great impact while at the same time having few or no staff and a small budget? Can you live a "successful" life if you've never had a career, a house, or a savings account?

Most of the people I have ministered to as a pastor over the last ten years do not have many of the things we think we need to have an abundant life. Most do not lead businesses or churches. Most don't own homes or have "assets" (whatever

8. *Magnum Force* (1973).

that means). Many are in debt and have little money to spend. A lot of them are low on organizational charts or aren't even on one to begin with. A great many of them were born without privileges of any kind. In fact, I would venture to say that most of you reading this fit these descriptions or something like them. We can't all be powerful, famous, and rich. But even if you are a leader, a boss, someone rich or influential or even famous—does this automatically mean your life is abundant? The overwhelming evidence within just our own experience would cause us to answer that question emphatically: *of course not.*

Business owners, entrepreneurs, and titans of industry are all certainly in our churches, and I have been pleased to interact with some of them. The ones who were filled with an abundant life had something else going on. There was another project—a side hustle of the soul—something in their life that had nothing to do with the kingdom they had set up themselves, and it was incredibly attractive. The path to a truly rich and abundant life has nothing to do with how much money you have and how much you have achieved. And that's mostly what I want to explore.

We all want a great life—the kind of life that could last forever. This is why Jesus came saying, "I came to give you life and life abundant" (cf. John 10:10). His message was (and is) not primarily for the rich, powerful, and influential. His message is available for *all.* There is no life too broken, too lost, too disassembled, too immoral, or too selfish for God to miraculously reclaim. Jesus proclaimed captives free and poor people blessed. He told those who are meek that the whole earth would one day be theirs. He was constantly giving people good news. And the early church carried out the same gospel: sight to the blind, the wanderer coming home, and the sick made well. And the primary facet of this gospel message that made it absurd and astounding was that all of these things were *for everyone*. The gates to this kind of abundant life were wide open. The places and spaces where God would give such a good life were not limited to poor people or rich people, or to the Jewish people or the Roman citizens. The Christian Scriptures put this right in front of our faces: *everyone's invited*.

I believe a good life—a truly abundant, thick, and rich kind of life—is available for every person on this earth. I just think it looks confusing and upside down when we first put it up against the common messages in American life. But what if these messages are wrong? What if the Great American Experiment of Living a Good Life is actually a failed one? That, my friends, would be good to know.

This is not some elongated Twitter rant or internet digression; rather, it is the attempt to recapture a vision we have lost—a biblical vision. The new (old) story—the counternarrative—is against so much of our America-trained minds. But we need a new outlook, a kind of outlook on life that is surprising, terrifying, and yet still remarkably abundant and full. I will spend the next two chapters trying to give you as big of a "flyover" of the story as possible. We will look at how our society has both "gained the world" and "lost its soul." From there, we will begin to weave both narratives together, seeking a new alternative. Wisdom seems to be calling to us from Scripture. It may be backward from all we've been taught as Western people, but I wonder, can we listen again to this story?

2

Gaining the World

And yet, the history of *this country* . . . from its *founding* . . .
we built on fantasy—on . . . an ideal of something rather
than on something we could prove.

A. M. HOLMES

When I was in college, my university bragged about being the *largest* public institution in the state. It never boasted about being the best. Perhaps they thought you'd come to such a conclusion yourself after hearing they were the biggest.

I wrote for the paper at that college right when most editors and publications were beginning to learn how articles could show up in a Google search.[1] When I brought my editor an idea for a story with a particular headline I liked,

---

1. This was just in 2008, if you can believe that. The internet was a very different space just ten years ago.

he replied, "It's a great story, but it won't Google for s**t."
It was the beginning of the clickbait world we live in now. It
was a good story, but we needed more clicks if we wanted
to grow the paper. And we did.

In high school and college, I worked in restaurants, and
it was all about sales—more food and more drinks ordered
means more money. Sell the dessert. Make sure to ask for a
second and third drink. Add the cheese and the avocado (you
always pay more for a good avocado in America).[2] More.
More. More.

It didn't seem strange, then, to be in my first job in full-
time Christian ministry and hear my pastor talk about opening a multimillion-dollar building. I did not need to reorient
my thinking or change my mind, because I was already well
versed in the American Story. We've got to grow—this is the
American way. And it was a good primer for what it would
feel like to live as an American Christian. I was nineteen.

Successful things grow, and great things get bigger. That's
how it works, I've been told. In the church, this meant more
people (who looked like us), a larger budget (for better equipment), a bigger building (for bigger productions), and more
staff (to get more people). These are the marks of a successful
church in America.

I watched my now-former pastor on the stage of this beautiful building we were about to open, telling all of us we were
sitting in a place that "testified to God's faithfulness." We
clapped. After a couple of months of the church growing,
the next five years included many people slowly leaving, the

2. I have learned to make my own avocado toast because some of my favor-
ites in San Francisco are running between $8 and $15 on any given day. That is,
unequivocally, too much for toast.

sanctuary becoming half-full, and big questions beginning to arise in my mind: *Is this the vision of Jesus? Is God faithful only when things increase and grow? Is he not faithful when the church loses money and people? Wouldn't God's sovereignty also include the decline of the churches he so chooses to decline?*

I kept tabs on this church through my friends who worked there and truly believed they were faithful people doing good work, but the budget was smaller and the attendance had shrunk. Had this church failed? Or was it simply in another season? Was this a good thing or a bad thing?

If we are following the American Story of More and More, it *has* failed—or is *currently* failing. And the focus now must be on how to make it grow again, get bigger, and "succeed."[3] That's the American Story I'm talking about.

The Voice in the Wilderness

But there is another story—another narrative—and it doesn't come from the epicenter of world economies, nor does it come from our tech companies or the leading intellectual hubs. Rather, this story—unlike the story of "more"—comes

3. In 2014, LifeWay Research released a study declaring "90% of Churches in America are in decline" and, therefore, "dying." Many headlines and blog posts were written that decried the American church. This happens a couple of times each year, and I've started to become bored by it. The truth is, the research *actually* claims that this 90 percent of churches are in decline "or growing at a pace slower than their community." That is a *very* important caveat. This means that if a church is in a fast-growing community but *not* matching the pace of the neighborhoods, then that church is in the 90 percent. And if a church is not growing at all but is in a neighborhood that is growing *slightly*, it is within that 90 percent of the "declining or dying." LifeWay did not sound the alarm bells, but plenty of pastors did. See Hefner, "8 Observations of a Revitalized Church."

from the margins, from the desert or the wilderness. It comes from the ghettos and the backcountry, the landscapes ignored by the internet, tourists, and content creators. This story comes from a voice crying "in the wilderness" (Isa. 40:3; Matt. 3:3).

And this new story had a messenger.

The messenger was just that—someone carrying something that wasn't his. He lived thousands of years ago and is referred to as "John the Baptizer." John, because that was his name, and "Baptizer," because that's what he spent his days doing—dunking people in water after they had changed their minds about the things mattering most in life.

He carried this message about someone greater than him who would come soon, a man who would be born a man, but also someone "whose sandals I am not worthy to untie" (Luke 3:16). That is to say, this man would be God, and his name would be Jesus.

This God-man, Jesus, "must increase," said John the Baptizer (John 3:30). John saw this as his mission, his emphasis: to help Jesus expand the scope of his ministry. He was obsessed with this. And this should still be the mission of modern churches—to "glorify" God or to make his name "greater." He *must* increase, John said.

The consequence of Jesus getting more honor, however, was simple. In John's own words, in order for Jesus to increase, "I must decrease."

I must decrease.

In John's mind, there was no way for Jesus to increase if "I" increase. There is no way for Jesus to be big if I am big. No way for him to grow if I grow. I've got to get small, slow, and ordinary if he will be big, quick, and extraordinary.

In the words of the nineteenth-century Scottish missionary Andrew Murray, "If I am something, then God is not everything."[4]

The voice in the wilderness is not a voice of innovation, excellence, and power. He is not a thought leader or a cultural entrepreneur. He doesn't have good ideas. Rather, he is a person of humility, obscurity, and obedience. This voice is not one of "upward mobility" but of downward mobility. What does this mean? Perhaps this means we should be suspicious of anything making us look bigger than we actually are. It could also mean we do not need to do as much as we think we should. Because how can Jesus be big if we're flexing our muscles? And how can he do something when we're already doing it in his place?

Decreasing in an Age of Increase

This message is not attractive to the modern American. We are, without question, the wealthiest group of people in the history of the world. Never before have we seen a nation with a larger GDP and economic growth. We have never had better health care, working conditions, and civil rights.

It is still true that we are nowhere near perfection, but take your class and job and status right now and ask yourself, "What era would I rather live in than this one?" I challenge you to think of a time in history where it was *better* to be poor, or a time throughout our nation's past where it was

---

4. Murray, *Absolute Surrender*, 95. Murray said this to a group of students preparing for ministry. His final chapter of this book, "An Address to Christian Workers," is less of a chapter and more of a sermon. The whole book is great, but the closing chapter is outstanding.

better to be disadvantaged, or sick, or working class. We live in the most privileged time in human history.

Technology has afforded us unbelievable abilities to get more work done from anywhere. Our phones are not phones—they are miniature computers connecting us to any piece of information within a matter of seconds. We can work and not be at work. And we can be entertained without having the hassle of Blockbuster or a movie theater.

Social media and streaming services have given us a wealth of pleasure and a feeling of connectedness. It is an unprecedented landscape of content and "people," although no one is really *there*. Music, movies, books, porn, newspapers, car dealership ads, comics, jokes, TV shows, articles, T-shirts, video games, filth, dictionaries, shopping malls—now add all of your friends to that and you have a good picture of the internet. We have everything right before us in the black mirror, just waiting to be turned on.

A more helpful question than "What do we have right now?" is actually "What do we *not* have right now?" The problem is not that we don't have enough; the problem is that we have no idea what we should do with all we *do* have. After constructing such an impressive country by all measurable standards, why would we slow down *now*?

The reason can be found in the raw numbers: we are not happy nor living fulfilling lives. As average household incomes have increased, so have the rates of depression.[5] In the

5. For average household income in the US, see Mislinski, "U.S. Household Incomes." For depression rates in the US, see Tavernise, "U.S. Suicide Rate Surges," and Collins, "Americans Are More Depressed." This case has been made many times over but never seems to settle in. There is a direct relationship in America between our economic growth and our depression rates. Likewise, children tend to be more depressed in wealthy areas than poor areas. Where I live, in the Silicon

last thirty years, our economy has grown at about the same rate our depression has grown (give or take 5 percent). Are these things connected? I'd like to entertain that question. We can be sure of this: *we have never had more than we do now, and we've never been more depressed about it.*

The Common Denominator of Unhappiness

It may come to your mind that the stats presented in the previous section were of those outside the church. But these figures do not represent "the church" or "the unchurched." This is America. And the shocking reality is that these numbers exist in our churches, all of which are filled with Americans fitting all of the aforementioned demographics.

Divorce, suicide, pornography, gun violence, theft, drugs, and depression all have similar or bigger numbers when studied within the church.[6] It's strange to think that the one thing uniting the churched and the unchurched is unhappiness. It is our common denominator.

The problem of having more than we've ever had and being more depressed than we've ever been is not a "worldly" problem or a "church" problem; it is a human problem particular to Western society. The churches we are a part of are all placed within this cultural landscape of plenty. All the while, the message remains: In spite of our abundance,

---

Valley near Stanford University, more teenagers attempt suicide per capita than anywhere else in our state, a statistic and story I will discuss more in chapter 9.

6. These statistics are, of course, not always accurate, because in order to study "Christians" the researchers rely on the participants to self-identify as Christians. When data is collected, many researchers take the participants' word for it, though many who call themselves "Christian" in a study rarely or never attend a local church. This flaw has been exposed in Wright, *Christians Are Hate-Filled Hypocrites . . . and Other Lies You've Been Told.*

let's go get more. Let's get bigger. Let's grow. Let's multiply profits.

But then we remember the voice of one crying in the wilderness, the voice of John the Baptizer calling us toward a new counter-narrative: *"I must decrease."*

The invitation to "decrease" flies in the face of our own mantra to increase. And this is just like the God of the Bible. There are laws by which human society, science, and business work. Laws like, "You're either growing or dying" and "Change or die." But God is a miraculous God—and by that I mean he suspends and bends the laws of our world to bring about its flourishing and healing. He's a God of redemption, who brings orphans back home and gives rebels access to his Spirit. He brings dead things to life, and he uses weak things to "shame the strong" and foolish things to embarrass "the wisdom of the world" (1 Cor. 1:18–31). God takes what we know "for sure" and questions it, shifts it, and remakes it. That which we deem "broken" he reassembles. The second law of thermodynamics is a kind of heresy, theologically. It says, "You can't unscramble an egg," but is this not precisely what God will do one day? He says emphatically: "Behold, I am making *all things new*" (Rev. 21:5, emphasis mine)![7]

7. For more, read Lewis, *Miracles*. Obviously, the second law of thermodynamics is true, and obviously this is an oversimplification of it. But as a theologian, I can't help but read all of the passages about God *physically* remaking the world and think about what that means for our general scientific laws. If one day, in the words of Samwise Gamgee, everything sad will come "untrue," then it seems that some of our physical laws will become untrue in the New Heavens and the New Earth. Not now, but one day. God is a God of the *miraculous*, and this means laws of science bend and break on his command. They are laws so long as the Lawmaker and Law-Sustainer keeps them in effect. "Those who believe in miracles are not denying that there is such a [scientific] norm or rule," writes Lewis. "They are only saying that it can be suspended. A miracle is by definition *an exception*. How can the discovery of the rule tell

The Size of Jesus' Way

But who cares about the voice of John the Baptizer? It's not like *he* was Jesus, or anyone of much importance. Just because he made up his mind to "decrease," does that mean we should as well? Certainly there exist plenty of other spiritual teachers and philosophers who thought differently. Also, the Bible is a big book. Why just pick this guy as the one to offer us a new calling and direction?

Well, first, John the Baptizer is not insignificant in the scope of human history. Jesus Christ said of him, "Of all who have ever lived, none is greater than John the Baptist" (Matt. 11:11 NLT). Jesus thought John was the greatest person alive. If the most important historical figure across all time says such a dramatically positive statement about John the Baptizer, we should probably give him a little more thought.

But second, and perhaps more convincing, the idea of *decreasing* and sticking to small, ordinary, and slow, faithful work is not just the idea of an itinerant preacher in the first century. Instead, it is laced throughout all of Scripture and found in Christian thinking throughout our history. The pursuit of the little things will, in the end, be our greatest human pursuit. Getting smaller always fills us up. The Bible tells this story throughout its entire contents.

Consider, too, the man John followed: Jesus. He founded no organization, traveled very few miles, lived a relatively short life, wrote no books, had limited financial resources, was rejected by his followers and peers, held no office, and

---

you whether, granted a sufficient cause, the rule can be suspended?" (*Miracles*, 72–73, emphasis mine).

yet remains the most influential person to have ever walked the earth. What does this say about what we deem important? Jesus died poor and betrayed by his friends and has still managed to be a model for how we should live our lives. Still, we tend not to listen to him.[8]

The more we chase after "more," the less we will get. But perhaps there are other things Jesus chased, taught, and discovered that we have yet to fully live into. This is most of what I desire to explore in this book. To chase our ambitious American dreams is to run through vapor expecting to hit solid rock—the expectation is asinine.

Could God be up to something in the unexplored margins of our society? Could the kingdom he is building be outside the central places of power? Maybe the message of God is not coming from Wall Street or Silicon Valley . . . maybe it's coming from the wilderness. The pursuit of Scripture, the pursuit of going lower and decreasing our platforms and opinions and bank accounts, might hold some deeper biblical ground than we think.

---

8. Dallas Willard often called Jesus "the smartest man in the world" (*The Divine Conspiracy*, 93). It's a fascinating articulation of divine omniscience put into human form. There is a temptation to dismiss a lot of biblical wisdom by calling it "archaic" or "ancient," as though that should dismiss any argument. But, as Tim Keller has pointed out, calling something a name is not a refutation of an argument. This is what C. S. Lewis called "chronological snobbery" (*Surprised by Joy*, 207), the idea that just because we live in a more advanced technological age, we can easily dismiss any confident statement of wisdom or knowledge from the ancients. There is, in fact, a Wikipedia entry on it that is brief and sufficient, but by no means exhaustive: https://en.wikipedia.org/wiki/Chronological_snobbery.

Losing Our Soul

The ship? Great God, where is the ship?

HERMAN MELVILLE, *Moby Dick*

The name of the neighborhood I worked in, "the Tenderloin," comes from its history of crime. San Francisco police officers in the early twentieth century would tell new recruits to head to this one square mile of the city where they were sure to make arrests—so many arrests, in fact, that they could afford a tenderloin cut of meat for their family that night. If you were ever short on arrests or tickets, you could always go to the Tenderloin.

The neighborhood is still the place in the city with the most crime, the most drug and sex traffic, and the highest concentration of homeless people. The ministry I worked for has been there for over thirty years, faithfully intervening on behalf of the people in the inner city. The work spans from a K–8 school, where kids wear crisp, white uniforms, to a thrift store reviewed favorably on the internet, to a daily rescue mission and a medical clinic.

When people first come to the neighborhood and are asked about their initial impressions, they often comment on the visible issues: drugs, homelessness, poverty, prostitution, uncleanliness, and so on. But the longer you stay in the Tenderloin, the more you realize all of these issues have roots. You stop being bothered by the smell of marijuana, urine, and crack, or the sight of a prostitute heckling a customer, and you start getting bothered by the loneliness. The surface-level stuff becomes sort of normal, and your attention starts going to what's beneath it all.

A Lonely, Lost Soul

This root of loneliness is best exposed if you were to enter one of the housing units near my old office. Many of the government-assisted apartment buildings or "hotels" include SROs—single-resident-occupancy units. These are small rooms with maybe a sink and a small hot plate and a community bathroom down the hallway. Some of these buildings are difficult to walk through, as trash and dead mice pollute the ground, while others are surprisingly well kept. Many people live alone in one room and keep to themselves all day and night. This environment reveals one of the root causes of all the addiction and crime in our neighborhood: isolation.

Isolation leads human beings to do things we would not do if we were surrounded by people who know us and care for us. It takes the best of us and makes us worse. It leads a person of integrity to be broken into fragments. It fans the flames of addiction. Remaining alone and without company is the primary way we lose our humanity.

In *Chasing the Scream*, journalist Johann Hari reworked the classic story our culture tells about addiction. The age-old story, Hari said, is that addiction is primarily genetic and must be penalized through prison sentences and misdemeanors. His research says otherwise. In "Everything You Think You Know about Addiction Is Wrong," his TED Talk based on the book, Hari summarizes one conclusion he made through his years of work: "The opposite of addiction is not sobriety. The opposite of addiction is connection."[1] Hari's point resonates with much of what I saw among the addicts in the Tenderloin and will be the subject of a later chapter. We use drugs like we use technology at times: to numb the pain of a lonely, lost soul. But drugs are the fruit and loneliness is the root.

Money and a Lost Soul

One of the many benefits, however, of working in an impoverished community like this is its inability to cover its worst sins and issues. Because of a lack of material and political resources, what you see is what you get. It is America laid bare. This is the opposite of wealthy communities.

---

1. This is one of those rare moments that I wish you were not reading this book and we were just sitting down in my living room talking, because I would stop our conversation and make you watch Hari's TED Talk. Also, I wish this link were "live," as they say, so you could just click on it and go there. Nevertheless, here's the link: https://www.ted.com/talks/johann_hari_everything_you_think_you_know _about_addiction_is_wrong.

Before I moved to San Francisco, I worked for ten years in the wealthier suburbs of Portland, Oregon, my hometown. There, in the polished communities of the metro area, money covered a multitude of sins. Addiction, lies, crime, and abuse went unseen because of the vast areas of land people owned, or the loose schedules and vague job descriptions they were able to hold in order to keep others at a distance from what we Americans absurdly call our "personal life." But there is no such thing as a personal life to someone who has no ability for privacy. That's the Tenderloin. And that is a lot of impoverished areas in our world.

When I worked in the Tenderloin, I would take the train from the Silicon Valley into the city every day. The train is a true train, not just a commuter rail or a subway. The Bay Area has the BART, which is more like a traditional big-city railway system. But the train is different. Because it travels through the Silicon Valley, most of the riders are wealthier tech-types and serious businesspeople. You can always tell who's rich by what shoes they're wearing, and the train had plenty of clean sneakers, fine leather shoes, and expensive high heels.

In the early days of riding the train, I noticed something striking as I was waiting on the platform. I would look down the line of people waiting, and I could not see one person who was not either staring at their phone, connected to their phone through headphones, or both. I stared for a long time. There were hundreds of people waiting for this train, and I just gazed at the diverse group, no one talking to each other. The platform was always silent.

I remember during my first days getting to know the people in the Tenderloin and thinking, *These people are so isolated,* and I felt terrible when I imagined how such isolation would impact them. And then I stared down that platform as we all waited for the same train. Nearly all of us standing there hunched over our phones had more money than anyone in the Tenderloin, but we had the same issue: we didn't know anybody. It seems you can gain the whole world and it still won't do a thing for your soul.

Well, how do you know those people are lonely? you may ask. *They may be reading a daily devotional or texting with a friend or reading an email from someone they love. They may be bored on the train and have many healthy relationships at work and home.* That's true, and I don't know if they're lonely or not. But I *do* know they're isolated. *We* are isolated.[2] You can't tell me that having your headphones in, blaring music, as you stare at a screen is telling the world, "I'm open and willing to engage with you!" This is why many women use earbuds as a first layer of protection against the danger of a creepy guy starting a conversation with them.[3]

Lonely or not—impoverished in the inner city or wealthy in the suburbs—there's a way to gain everything and still not have it. This is what Jesus meant when he said, "For what does it profit a man to gain the whole world and forfeit his soul?" (Mark 8:36). Money does not fulfill a lost, lonely soul; it just hides it.

---

2. Also, just be patient until chapter 5, when isolation is my main subject. If you're not convinced now, allow me to try to convince you in the pages ahead.

3. One thing I could not stop thinking about in my commute through the city was how different my experience was as a man compared to my fellow commuters who were female. I often saw young women gawked at and catcalled as they walked through the city. It was not uncommon to see men just staring, too.

In his novel *Freedom*, Jonathan Franzen writes about Patty, a middle-class woman from the typical Midwestern suburban background. She lives the American Story with remarkable predictability. After graduating from the University of Minnesota, she marries her college boyfriend, who gets a great job; they buy a good house and settle down with two kids. But when Patty grows to be middle aged, she becomes incurably restless. While fixing up a family cabin in the woods, she begins an extramarital affair, thinking it would help her experience some new form of happiness and excitement for life. But instead she spirals into a depression. Patty becomes confused: she's gotten everything she's wanted all the time for most of her life, but she's never felt more deserted and unhappy. Franzen writes: "Where did the self-pity come from? The inordinate volume of it? By almost any standard, she held a luxurious life. She had all day every day to figure out some decent and satisfying way to live, and yet all she ever seemed to get for all her choices and all her freedom was more miserable. . . . She pitied herself for being so free."[4]

The more we get, the less we get, it seems. For all the privilege money buys us, for all the freedom we seemingly have to do what we want, we're still stuck with "us," and the escape seems impossible. This chapter will be (most likely) the hardest to read. My desire is to show how, amidst a culture of material abundance, we are *spiritually impoverished*. And I hope to show you this in a new way, with fresh considerations. This is where we hear the bad news, but I promise there's a compelling vision for our souls coming.

4. Franzen, *Freedom*, 181.

Maybe there's little difference between the line of young, rich people on their phones waiting for the train and the lines of SRO apartments in the Tenderloin. Through our phones and social-media feeds, we simply create for ourselves our own small room with our own things in it where no one else will touch us and from which the dangers of the unknown world will be cut off. We are glorified shut-ins, hermits with electronic lives making us appear "social," all while we ignore the massive city filled with human beings just outside our door. I'm telling you, money hides a multitude of sins.

Sin as Epidemic

What are "the multitude of sins"? This multitude is worse than sexual promiscuity or material greed because it is deeper than these manifestations. The expansion of "sin" in our time is *not* behavioral; it is spiritual. "Sin" is greatly different from "sins." The Sin (capital S) of the world is not moral misdeeds but is the root of moral misdeeds. It is the cancer in the bloodstream of the human race, the fracture at the bottom of every person, the misalignment of the universe. Sin is far bigger than who we sleep with; *it's who we are.*

The losing of the American soul is a problem of Sin, not sins. The "sins" we see are a result of the great disease (Sin) with which we are plagued, and which we cannot expunge by ourselves. Fleming Rutledge uses the metaphor of sin as a disease with great effect, saying, "the equally fallen created order are sick unto death beyond human resourcefulness."[5]

5. Rutledge, *The Crucifixion*, 141. Rutledge is also one of many pastor-theologians to make the distinction between "sins" and "Sin" (with a capital S). So much so that her book includes a detour to explain the difference. I'll

Even the sins we do not think are "that bad" or those we commit unwittingly are like cancer, "invasive, infecting, growing with almost organic inevitability."[6] Sin is when we look at the world to realize it is "not the way it's supposed to be."[7]

And it's deeper than that: it's when we see the world not as it should be, and then each decision we make to try to right it messes it up again. Like the farmers who found a pesticide to help their soybeans grow only to completely undercut the population of honeybees, one decision helps us as it simultaneously hurts us in another way we could never foresee.[8] This is Sin. The world we have broken is impossible for us to put back together, because the problem is not so much "the world" or "the culture"; the problem, again, is *us*.

Enlarging our vision of sin to "Sin" with a capital *S* is done here not to shame us, but to place us in a position of desperation, perfectly suited to receive grace. The path to abundant life must begin in a recognition that while "we live in a beautiful world,"[9] we also live in one filled with loneliness, poverty, injustice, exhaustion, and helplessness.

---

recommend this book to you—that is, if it already hasn't been done. Rutledge's theology of the cross is the most comprehensive and engaging since John Stott's *The Cross of Christ*.

6. Radner, *Leviticus*, 63.

7. This phrase, and the metaphor of disease/cancer, is found in Cornelius Plantinga Jr.'s *Not the Way It's Supposed to Be*, which is still, in my opinion, the best book on sin. It's brief, highly accessible, and seemingly timeless. I hope that book is read one hundred years from now.

8. The declining population of honeybees worldwide was linked to the safety of neonicotinoids, a pesticide used to help grow corn and soybeans, two massive industries in US farming. The mass death of honeybees in 2015 caused even the president to get involved; he created a task force on pollination in order to right the ship. See Wines, "A Sharp Spike in Honeybee Deaths Deepens a Worrisome Trend."

9. Coldplay, "Beautiful World," *Parachutes* (Parlophone, 2000).

Sin runs deeper than the "sins." Sin runs in our blood and leads us to live unconnected, busy lives of which we may come to the end only to say, "I now see that I spent most of my life doing neither what I ought nor what I liked."[10] We have not lost our souls because of our morality; we have lost our souls because we have convinced ourselves we are like God and not headed for death. We are proud, fat, anxious; ultimately, sick. And so, through our screens and careers and obsessions, we have begun to medicate ourselves. Let's do a quick flyover to see how that has been working for us.

Connected and Alone

The internet has proven to be a perfect, brief salve for our Sin. Ever felt lonely and opened your phone? Ever been sad and turned to a screen? It's the natural place for us to go to feel *some* kind of connection, even if we're still alone in our room.

If you were to have told me when I was thirteen that you had every song ever made in your basement, and you invited me there, my reply would have been, "Go there? Can I live there?" Well, this hypothetical basement *is* the internet— where the whole world fits in our pockets. Any piece of information, any song, most movies or television shows, book titles, recipes, and celebrity photos all can be accessed. Even more, we can publish ourselves and let everyone know just what we want them to know about us and how wonderful we are through our various means of social connection. As I type this, there are more than two billion people on Facebook,

10. Lewis, *The Screwtape Letters*, 23.

along with 974 million Twitter profiles. This is why I will often turn off my Wi-Fi when I write. There's just too much out there, and none of it is real.

Has the total access to the entire world made us better people? It's hard to give any answer other than no. Instead of providing a vast, democratic landscape of free information, social media and the comments section of any article have not grown us to be more empathetic, but more villainous. What some envisioned as a shared "third space" for open conversation is now a bloodbath where anonymous users launch pathetic insults garnished with grammatical errors and misspellings.

The British journalist Jon Ronson spent years investigating the stories of people whose lives were ruined through online public shaming. In his book on the subject, *So You've Been Publicly Shamed*, Ronson quotes a long email from his friend, the documentary filmmaker Adam Curtis, who wrote, "The tech utopians . . . present [the internet] as a new kind of democracy. . . . It isn't. It's the opposite. It locks people off in the world they started with and prevents them from finding out anything different. They get trapped in the system of feedback reinforcement. Twitter passes lots of information around. But it tends to be the kind of information that people know that others in their particular network will like."[11]

11. Ronson, *So You've Been Publicly Shamed*, 280. Ronson's book explores the dark underside of social media, and he pulls no punches by involving all of us in the evil. What I love about this book—and there's so much to love—is Ronson's ability to prove how this is not a problem on the outside, but on the inside. Internet shaming is not something bad people do; it's something all of us desire to do. No matter how big or small of a role we think we play, we (and Ronson includes himself) all desire justice on our own terms, where other people are given consequences and we are seen as righteous. For someone who rejects Christianity, he provides a very good picture of what we Christians know to be universal sin.

While we originally hoped the internet would open our minds, it has only showed us how closed they really are. Recommended friends to follow and suggested purchases from frequently visited websites "randomly" popping up in our feeds are the harmless manifestations, but the echo chamber of news, information, and commentary within our social media feeds becomes the danger. This is why I was surprised by the results of the 2016 presidential election. No one on *my* internet would have voted for Trump . . . so how could he ever win?[12]

The internet (and the various technologies that surround it) has not given us any more possession of the world, or of anything else for that matter. We have not gained anything, and we have not grown. We have shrunk. We have lost something. We have more information than ever but very little soul or heart. We hold all of the information from millions of books in our pockets, but we have no wisdom. The more stories we hear, the less empathetic we get, and the courage we need to stand up to misuses of power will be thwarted as we convince ourselves that tweeting about it is just as good, when it clearly is not.

I absolutely affirm and understand the various ways technology has made our lives better. I love Twitter and have seen the massive benefits of a more technologically connected

12. After the election of Donald Trump, many of the best progressive minds tried sorting through why or how it could have happened. Perhaps most convincing and intimate was David Remnick's interview with Barack Obama. Remnick followed Obama and his closest aides the night of the election and wrote about it in the *New Yorker*. In the piece, Remnick interviews David Simas, Obama's political director, who reflected on the "barriers" of discourse coming down in the era of social media. "This creates a whole new permission structure," he said, "a sense of social affirmation for what was once thought unthinkable. This is a foundational change." Much ink was spilled on the internet's relationship to the election results without really anyone on the liberal side of politics saying what all were thinking: we were wrong. Remnick, "Obama Reckons with a Trump Presidency."

world. Uber and Lyft give us safer, more affordable means of transportation; FaceTime connects us more intimately with those who are far from us. But it still seems to be clear now that the internet has not done what we hoped it would. We saw it as a landscape of endless opportunity and knowledge. We thought it would make our kids smarter and our workers more efficient. We thought it would make us more open than ever, but it's currently making us more closed off than we were before, just in a different way. We no longer have to have a conversation with someone while we wait for the bus. Instead of the internet being the opening we needed to connect the world, much of it has given us the ability to isolate ourselves from it.

When given the ability to expand goodness and justice and wisdom through the internet, we instead use it to outcast people in our society. Technology is not the problem; our use of it is. The internet is an innocent tool we use, and it just so happens to expose our wickedness.

We don't use things correctly. We have more technology than any previous generation and have been able to use such technology for further evidence of our Sin. The more we get, the more we lose. And so when we feel sad about our phones and technology, we convince ourselves that our career paths will give us the meaningful life we feel we deserve. If technology cannot distract us from our Sin, certainly our jobs could try.

Working and Exhausted

Most Americans cannot afford to take a weekend off. Research shows Americans take an average of 16.2 days off a year, down from twenty-one days off in 2000.[13] And this doesn't count when we're out of the office but logged in to our email. It's now a badge of honor to be on vacation and "not looking at my email all week." Even if we really do, on average, take sixteen days off a year, how many of those days are we still mostly plugged in to our addiction to work?

Compared to nations like Italy, which requires office and factory workers to take at least a month off every year, the United States is the only advanced country without mandatory vacation or federally supported maternity leave.[14] If you're a new mom, you've got to keep building the nation—no breaks or vacations. Many moms in America take just two weeks off after the baby is born and then put their newborn into day care and get back to work.

In a 2014 issue of the *New Yorker*, Elizabeth Kolbert reviewed a book by *Washington Post* reporter Brigid Schulte entitled *Overwhelmed: Work, Love, and Play When No One Has the Time*. In the review, Kolbert began by telling us about another article written by the economic philosopher John Maynard Keynes before the Depression, the Second World War, and the sexual and postmodern revolution.

In his 1920s article titled "Economic Possibilities for Our Grandchildren," Keynes predicted that through technological

13. Neighmond, "Overworked Americans."

14. The best special series NPR has done in my lifetime is "Stretched: Working Parents' Juggling Act," which covered in great detail the absurd injustice of paternal and maternal leave in America. I would challenge you to listen to these stories of real women and men struggling to not just "raise children" but give basic care to a newborn—and they're not the poorest of the poor. Many hardworking women take vacation time or unpaid leave in order to care for their one-week-old child. It is not uncommon in America for women to take two weeks' vacation and be back to work while their three-week-old goes to a form of day care. This goes against all of the research done by pediatricians and developmental psychologists. For more on the series, see NPR, "Stretched."

advancement and economic growth, his grandchildren (which would be us, by the way) would be able to have an increased amount of leisure. His prediction went even further, suggesting that our generation, the workforce of the new millennium, would have three-hour workdays and produce twice as much as they were in the 1930s. Three-hour workdays—that's fifteen hours a week. Can you imagine?

Just before Keynes submitted this essay for publication in 1929, the stock market crashed. Although much changed between the time he wrote it and when it was published, Keynes did not waver. He said—in a classic macroeconomic and Keynesian way—that this was just a bump in the road, that our future still looked rosy, that at the end of it all, his grandchildren would still work way less and produce way more. Kolbert concluded the review by reflecting back on Keynes's proposition: "It is, to say the least, disappointing that things haven't turned out that way—that inequality has grown, that leisure is scarce, that even the rich complain of being overwhelmed. And yet so much of what we do, collectively and individually, suggests that we still believe more wealth is the answer. Reexamining this belief would probably be a good idea—that is, if anyone had the time for it."[15]

We've built the very machine to which we have become a slave. This is the kind of work that builds large, powerful, and secure economies. But this is not the kind of work that builds a soul. Our jobs distract us, our paychecks provide funds for our vices, and we learn to be amicable in the workplace so we might get rewards of bonuses and extra time off. It seems like all we get for all we do is more of the same.

15. Kolbert, "No Time."

Satisfaction in life cannot come from the *inside* of our careers or technology; it can only come from the *outside*.

Living While Dead

The great tragedy and sadness is that all of this gain appears to have left us empty. It's even leaving us for dead. The statistics are sobering. More kids have committed suicide in the last fifteen years than the previous forty combined. The rate of young people on antidepressants or antianxieties has tripled in the past twenty years. There is an opioid epidemic, with people of all ages painfully addicted to medications meant to take pain *away*. Gun violence and murder rates are at an all-time high among young people, and young adults between the ages of twenty-one and twenty-four are more likely to die in a drunk-driving accident than by almost any other cause of death.[16] And if you're black and between the ages of fifteen and thirty-four, your most likely cause of death is homicide.[17]

The Center for Disease Control noted a 24 percent increase in the suicide rate since 1999, with a greater rate of increase after 2006.[18] Between just 2009 and 2012, the rate

16. For all of our discussion on drunk driving, and all of the various programs to draw young Americans' attention to the massive fatality rates, CBS News was still led to ask, "Could 2016 be the worst year for drunk driving deaths?" Their answer? Basically, yes: see Van Cleave, "2016 May Go Down as One of the Worst Years for Drunk-Driving Deaths."

17. The increasing number of homicides among young black men—and the subsequent ignoring of this fact by the media and government—is chronicled in Jill Leovy's remarkable book *Ghettoside*. It is unfortunately outside of the scope of this book to go into greater detail on this important subject. Thankfully, Leovy has.

18. See Curtin, Warner, and Hedegaard, "Increase in Suicide in the United States, 1999–2014."

of depression among people older than twelve jumped by 7.6 percent.[19] I have no scientific evidence to prove this next thought, but do you find it interesting that suicide rates climbed just as Facebook (which debuted in 2006) and other social media sites took off? There was enough content glorifying or advocating self-harm on the social media site Tumblr that they took the step of banning it in 2012.[20]

My friend Vickie is a nurse and often uses her training and gifting to lead youth camps. We were leading one back in Oregon with about three hundred suburban middle-school kids. She was unloading all of the medications, remarking on how many of these twelve-year-olds were on antidepressants. At the time, she was living in Baltimore and working in the inner city. "There are always more kids on antidepressants from the suburbs," she said. I've been thinking about this ever since I heard it six years ago.[21]

Who Is Really Well-Off?

This may prove to be a depressing chapter. But I have organized the book in such a way that the worst is, in my opinion, behind us. Having an appropriate understanding of our relationship with Sin and the loneliness of our souls will provide the perfect landing strip for grace to enter our culture. As Americans, we believe ourselves to be well-off—and we may

19. See Centers for Disease Control and Prevention, "Depression."

20. Tumblr, "A New Policy against Self-Harm Blogs."

21. For a detailed and interesting history of depression in the United States and beyond, read Whitaker, *Anatomy of an Epidemic*. Whitaker says of the movement to create one pill to cure depression: "The psychopharmacology revolution was born from one part science and two parts wishful thinking" (47). A lot of Whitaker's argument boils down to the pharmaceutical wish that you can take a pill for everything. Placing this in the context of mental illness has seen disastrous results.

very well be in some ways. But we are mostly well-off materially or economically. My argument through this chapter is to reveal how we are not well-off *spiritually* and that this fact has massive societal and cultural consequences.

Nevertheless, the biblical authors know how neediness connects us to God, and how he "opposes the proud but gives grace to the humble" (James 4:6). To be weak, poor, and needy is to be ripe and ready for God's activity in your life. But material advantages breed spiritual disadvantages. We must regain an understanding of our neediness if our souls are to be filled with the grace of God.

Moving from suburban youth ministry to working in the inner city of San Francisco, this became all the more clear throughout my ministry life. People from wealthy areas were just as depressed—statistically, *more* depressed—as the under-resourced and materially poor people in vulnerable communities like the Tenderloin. So why are we convinced we're actually living?

Nearly all of us who have worked with the poor can testify to how they continually teach us the happiness and joy found even when you have very few material items. But we rarely reflect on how difficult it is to find joy when we have *a lot* of material items.

The New Testament teaches that to be rich is to be spiritually disadvantaged. If you are poor, Jesus calls you "blessed." Dallas Willard says the term "blessed" is best understood as the answer to the question "Who is well-off?" or "Who has the good life?"[22] Jesus agonized over the rich, saying they are *not* the blessed ones. "How difficult it is for those who have

---

22. Willard, *The Divine Conspiracy*, 97.

wealth to enter the kingdom of God!" he exclaimed (Luke 18:24). But to the poor, Jesus said, "Yours is the kingdom of God" (Luke 6:20). To be poor is to have a spiritual advantage. Those who have materially less have greater access to spiritual things. Perhaps this makes Americans spiritually handicapped.

John the Baptizer was right. Maybe in all of our increasing, our Jesus has been decreasing. As we increase our self-sufficiency, we have seen a decrease in the activity of God. Maybe just living in America has blinded us to the reality seen from heaven: God is everything. The massive nature of God is lost when we convince ourselves of how big we think we are.

We, then, are like the hoarders in the inner city living in small SRO apartments: convincing ourselves everything in our space matters. There's not much of a difference between the poor and the rich. We are both now in need of changing our desire to become as big as a god. We must reject the idea of being everything if we want God to be something. We—both inside our churches and outside—must abandon our pursuit of endless expansion and increase for this very simple, very profound reason: *it's not working.*

What's Next?

As I charted out in the first chapter, the narrative for Americans begins with the worship of growth and ends in a pile of money atop which one can retire. Christians are given another story, a counter-narrative, from John the Baptizer, Jesus, and the Scriptures. Our story is one of pace, humility, suffering, vulnerability—all ending in glory. To ignore the call of the Scriptures would not only be foolish, but I believe it is life-threatening. As I've tried to emphasize in this chapter, this is not just about being "good Christians"; our lives are at stake.

The work ahead of us in this book will be to hear the call from our Western cultures to "increase" and pit it against its opposite. This will help us see the counter-narrative, the new story for Christians in the twenty-first century. I will look at concepts like "growth" (how everything we do should get bigger faster) and compare it with "pace" (how everything we do should get to its proper size during its proper time). We will look at things like "isolation" (attempting more through self-sufficiency) and pit it against "connection" (attempting less in order to form meaningful relationships). I will do the same with concepts like "fame versus obscurity" and "power versus vulnerability." We will see the story of America come into contact with the call of Jesus and work to see how we can live faithful lives in a culture of luxury, increase, and pride.

My hope is that by holding these cultural concepts next to one another, we might understand which one to err toward. I say "err toward" because the answer to these concerns will not be in extremes—the truth is rarely found there. Instead, we will find the truth where the Scriptures see it: in subtlety, nuance, and paradox. There, in the hard work of questioning our assumptions, we will find what every human has ever been looking for: a life of great abundance.

PART 2

You Were Probably Right

4

Growth and Pace

I did think, let's go about this slowly.
This is important. This should take
Some really deep thought. We should take
Small thoughtful steps.
But, bless us, we didn't.

MARY OLIVER, "I Did Think,
Let's Go About This Slowly"

You'll be surprised how much truth there is in a taqueria. Steps away from my apartment, just past the law offices and dive bar, there's a little taco place. My wife and I enjoy their takeout quite a bit: fish tacos, veggie burritos, carne asada, and homemade chips have all become mainstays as we answer the routine question "What do you want to eat tonight?" The man and woman who run the place (I have never seen anyone else operate it) are efficient while also being exceptionally generous, warm, and hospitable. It's something to admire. They are some of the hardest-working people I know.

Many days, I walk my dog at 5:00 a.m. It's not my favorite time of day to walk around, but I need to be up early in order to get to work on time. When I walk by the taqueria, I always see the same woman inside making chips and tortillas for the day—at 5:00 a.m. I never beat her to the morning—she's always there before me, no matter the hour, it seems. It's also common to see the man and woman enjoying a beer or soda behind the counter after the place has closed for the night. The TV is running a soccer game or something, and for a second you think they're open, but they're not. They're enjoying a good day's work. They work hard six days a week with long hours, and they're closed only on Sundays and holidays.

My first year living here, I was in my daily routine of walking my dog when I noticed, on a Monday afternoon, the taqueria was closed. There was a small handwritten sign stuck on the glass door, taped on from the inside. For a second I thought they may be shutting down. God have mercy—*Where would I get my tacos?*

The note simply read: "We will be closed December 25–January 7 to enjoy time with our family and rest. See you when we return." This is the type of gift that can only be given to us by someone outside of the American Story. The rejection of "the machine" and the embrace of relationships. This is an understanding of pace.

The taqueria is a Silicon Valley business. This little taco place is ten minutes from Facebook's never-closing office and twenty-five minutes from the Googleplex. They are successful. They make enough money. And certainly someone has told them, "You guys make amazing tacos. You should sell. You should expand. You should open another taqueria and make more money. You should be open *seven* days a week." And this person, if they exist, might be enraged or confused as to why the owners would close for two weeks in the middle of "the holiday season" to "enjoy time with family and rest." The average American thinks, *Why would you do that when you could hire other people and make more money?*

And yet, is there something these taqueria owners understand that the Silicon Valley does not? Could their use of the word "no" leave them open to say yes to things we're missing out on? Could there be wisdom and knowledge in this little taqueria that can help the Silicon Valley billionaires learn more about what it means to be happy? These taco-making business owners know something we often ignore: enough is enough.

American Growth

The journalist Sam Quinones spent over ten years outside of America, in Mexico, writing and reporting on the drug war for the *Los Angeles Times*. His time away was during the late 1990s and early 2000s, when many of our technological advances were taking place. After he arrived back in the States, he noticed "a scary obesity emerging." And he didn't just mean our waistlines. "Everything seemed obese and excessive," he wrote. "Massive Hummers and SUVs were cars on steroids. In some of the Southern California suburbs near where I grew up, on plots laid out with three-bedroom houses in the 1950s, seven-thousand-square-foot mansions barely squeezed between the lot lines, leaving no place for yards in which to enjoy the California sun."[1] For those of us who grew with America, nothing seems out of the ordinary, but to those outside looking in the question is simple: *Don't you have enough?*

Conservatives and liberals in the West have infused our culture with a kind of addiction to growth over the past fifty to sixty years. President Ronald Reagan convinced voters it was "Morning in America," the dawn of a period of vast and expansive economic growth. Bill Clinton's secretary of the treasury, Lawrence Summers, said the Democrats "cannot and will not accept any 'speed limit' on American economic growth. It is the task of economic policy to grow the economy as rapidly . . . as possible."[2] In the 2016 election, both Hilary Clinton and Donald Trump jousted about who could grow the economy faster.[3] No one wins elections in America by saying "I think we have enough."

Our culture is so inundated with the "More is better" mentality that it is difficult to see it unless we step outside of it for a while. A couple of years ago, when my wife and I traveled to Turkey, I remember noticing how little their tea and coffee cups were—nothing like the Starbucks "Venti" to be seen (except, of course, at Starbucks).[4] Meal portions in

1. Quinones, *Dreamland*, 37. This is an incredibly fascinating book on the opioid epidemic in America, tracing the story from its strange, alarming roots of misinformation and all-too-quick thinking by pseudo experts. Physicians and pharmacists are still picking up the garbage. If you would like to understand the opioid epidemic in America, this book is essential.

2. These quotes and this concept are from Bill McKibben's excellent book *Deep Economy*, 8–10.

3. See the Associated Press, "Here's How Trump and Clinton Each Say They Would Ignite Economic Growth."

4. Starbucks used to offer only one drink size: "tall." It is now the smallest before the "kid size" option.

many other countries could not even pass as an appetizer at most American restaurants.

It is not rare for Americans to have a "spare room" or an extra car—do we understand just how rare this is across the world? Our lives are so inoculated with growth, excess, and increase that we hardly even know it is happening. If we can buy two for one, we'll do it—*Why wouldn't we?* If we can get more for less, why would we not get more? It seems that when Costco is our normal grocery store, everything changes.

This is the culture in which our churches exist as well. This is the water we are swimming in. And perhaps this is why we never question our pastors when they say, "We must grow the church!" It seems right to us—*Why wouldn't it be better if it were bigger?*

The Pressure of Growth

Like the Silicon Valley billionaires, not many churches know what the taqueria owners in my neighborhood know. To shut down, to slow up, to give pace to ministry or business is difficult for American Christians. We celebrate "the fastest-growing churches in America." *Outreach* magazine devotes a special issue each year, and a whole section of their website, to their annual list of the one hundred fastest-growing churches.[5] We are fascinated by churches that grow seemingly overnight, and we listen to those who have hired more staff than we have over the course of three years.

When churches do not grow, we question leadership. When we do not expand, buy property, or move to a third gathering,

5. See *Outreach*, "Outreach 100." The only thing that seems to generate similar fanfare is when they publish the list of the *largest* churches in America.

we wonder what's wrong. The staff may begin to form theories about it, and the youth pastor believes that if they only had younger voices on Sunday they would grow. All over America, pastors from all levels of all churches are pulled into offices and questioned about why their church or ministry has not grown. Especially the youth and children's pastors. Is this right?

The truth is, it's not hard to grow a church's attendance, and it's not too difficult to raise money. What is hard, though, is pastoring a church, shepherding it. But we have exchanged shepherding churches for growing them. And I'm afraid we're reaping what we've sowed.

The End of the Megachurch

The megachurch is a relatively new invention. Certainly we have instances dating back to the book of Acts and the Great Awakenings that include descriptions of large *gatherings*, but large and local congregations with massive stadium-like buildings are a relatively recent development in our religious landscape.

Between 1994 and 2004, a record number of congregations had a weekly attendance of over two thousand, which is what deems them, statistically, a "megachurch." Crossing into the twenty-first century, there have never been more large churches in American history. Because of this seemingly tremendous growth, we might be led to believe that American Christianity is thriving. And yet "nearly every major statistical survey into American church life is showing that the nation is becoming less and less churched, even as megachurches become bigger and bigger."[6] What happened? What we learn from a dive into the statistics of megachurches is simple: while American Christian congregations balloon in size, the church across the nation has experienced a net loss.

Additionally, studies by Christian Schwartz and others have shed light on the fact that megachurches tend to exist in affluent suburbs, are predominantly found in the Bible Belt and the Sun Belt, and see most of their growth from "transfer growth," or Christians coming to the megachurch from other churches.[7]

We are far enough along to see statistics of the American megachurch movement and deem it a questionable success in church history. Perhaps more accurately and softly, we can more confidently say the average American megachurch is certainly not *necessarily* successful. Large churches that contain fruitful ministry of new life have something else going on. Not all megachurches are successful in the eyes of God, and smaller churches should take note. Bigness does not equal greatness.

I'm reminded of a megachurch pastor, Rick Warren, who famously says of churches, "Bigger is not better, smaller is not better; better is better."[8] I deeply admire leaders like Warren, who use their platform to communicate a central message: just because they're the biggest doesn't mean they're the best. These churches, despite having grown quickly and remaining large, have learned the art of pace.

6. Wilson, *The Prodigal Church*, 35. The statistics quoted here are also taken from the second chapter of Wilson's book.

7. This data is summarized nicely in Wilson, *The Prodigal Church*, 25–46.

8. Papa Rick, as many of his church members know him, has said this a lot, but is quoted most clearly and recently in Rainer, "2014 Update on Largest Churches in the Southern Baptist Convention."

And still, our default is toward growing everything bigger. It just seems right to us as Americans. Church planters are still considered "failing" if their church cannot grow above one hundred people on a Sunday, and the little church on the edge of town or the tiny inner-city church is seen as "struggling" if their numbers remain the same week to week. What's the solution?

"Healthy Things Grow"

"Healthy things grow" is a common phrase in church leadership.[9] This is often painted as the measure for a church's success—it's all about health. You will hear it at conferences and read it in books defending numerical growth. The principle is simple: if your church is healthy, it will grow. More people will come to a healthy church than an unhealthy church. But people still come to unhealthy churches. Often, our measurement of "health" means more "organizationally sound" than other churches we see: the systems are clean and the processes to get things done happen quickly and efficiently. Most use the phrase to talk about numerical growth. But the Bible's conception of a "healthy" thing is that it bears fruit while connected to Christ, and I think bearing fruit looks a lot more diverse than more butts in our seats.

I don't think there's anything wrong with a healthy church decreasing in size and even dying. Don't some local churches serve their season and just . . . end? Just because an orga-

---

9. Putting "healthy things grow" and "church" into a Google search will provide pages of blog posts by Christian leaders and pastors, mostly agreeing with this epitaph, save for the great Larry Osborne, who questions it in a remarkable post titled "The Myth of Endless Growth."

nization exists for a long time or gets large does not mean it's "healthy." Plastic is one of the hardest things to destroy, and while there are a lot of adjectives for it, "healthy" is not one.

It's true, healthy things *do* grow. But healthy things also eventually die. Healthy plants still need pruning. The forest still sets itself on fire for long-term sustainability. And doesn't cancer grow and spread too? What about bacteria or a virus? Destruction grows just as much as life.[10]

Sometimes unhealthy churches get bigger. Sometimes healthy churches stay around the same size because they're planted in transient cities where young people come and go. Sometimes things aren't that clean and churches are not "healthy" or "unhealthy"; they're in a grayer area where there might be transition or instability for a short while, but there's no reason to panic.

Sometimes ministry isn't that neat. Oftentimes it is chaotic. And still, work is done, people are baptized, cities are served, children are protected, and disciples are made. The realm of ministry activity—or what Jesus called "the kingdom of God"—still sees results. We still see some things in God's kingdom, but it doesn't look like the things in Silicon Valley's kingdom. How can Jesus lead us to a definition of "success"?

Jesus' Agricultural Language

When he spoke about the kingdom of God, Jesus told little stories, or "parables." He told these stories, it seems, because

10. Wilson, *The Prodigal Church*, 40.

he could not or did not want to describe this "kingdom" in a sentence. We, too, should be careful to avoid doing so.[11] If Jesus did not neatly define the kingdom of God in a short sentence, what makes us think we can?

There are no "principles" for the kingdom of God, nor are there solid definitions. Jesus gave us *metaphors*. Through his images, we see the truth he was speaking of—if we have "ears to hear," that is (Matt. 11:15).[12] Stories are not given to us to extrapolate, but to absorb, take in, and cherish. We must approach Jesus' parables with a similar humility, avoiding "categorization." My hope in the following section is to stay away from such dissections and instead simply inflate or magnify these already beautiful stories. Let's stare then, for a second, into these pictures.

Nearly all of Jesus' parables about the kingdom of God are agricultural. His stories start with farmers, seeds, trees, soils, hired hands, plows, and land. For twenty-first-century Americans to think we can read these stories once and "get the gist of it" would be arrogant and naive. Speaking for myself and also for many others who are distant from such environments: we need help. It's difficult to cherish metaphors with which we do not connect.

And still, we *must* connect with Jesus' images—they cannot be replaced. He told us these stories to communicate something deeply true about humankind and life with God.

11. Unless you're Dallas Willard.

12. Jesus frustrated his followers with his answer as to *why* he spoke in parables (Matt. 13:10–17; Mark 4:10–20; Luke 8:9–15). It seems as though Jesus found stories to be the best way to communicate the deep, transcendent realities of what he referred to as his "kingdom." Many authors of novels resonate with this when they are asked the ridiculous question of explaining their book or telling an audience somewhere "what it's really about." Most writers will shake their head and say, "It's in the pages." For more, see McFague, *Speaking in Parables*.

For us to swap out "farmers" for "employees" and "plows" with "phones" will cause us to miss the very things he wants us to see. These stories are not easily replaced or recast. We must follow his lead. What do we need to know about Jesus' agricultural pictures?

First, agriculture is *slow*. There is nothing quick about a seed. Jesus tells us his kingdom is like a seed planted in the ground, "but when it has grown it is larger than all the garden plants and becomes a tree" (Matt. 13:32). Do you know how long it takes to grow a tree? I'll give you a hint: it's longer than a Sunday service or a small-group session. Planting requires patience, and apparently so does the kingdom of God. Jesus' images involve a process that can only be described as *painstakingly slow*. If God's pace is like this, how does that change our approach to ministry and life with him?

Second, agriculture is *dependent on outside forces*. There is no such thing as an independently successful farmer. Any farmer with a measure of success has a rich relationship with the land and the environment and sees those things as equally responsible for his work. Some winters are good, some are not. Droughts sometimes stick around for much longer than you would think. Even the best equipment can't withstand a tornado. At the end of the day, a farmer only produces results *in partnership* with the weather conditions. God's kingdom is a lot like this. There are outside forces that can lead the best ministers into great peril or the worst into rich success. Not everything is up to our ingenuity and expertise; some things happen *to us* from the outside. We do not fight a battle of "flesh and blood" (Eph. 6:12). Jesus' brother James wrote about these first two aspects of agriculture and the kingdom toward the end of his profound letter, saying, "Be patient, therefore, brothers, until the coming of the Lord. See how the farmer waits for the precious fruit of the earth, being patient about it, until it receives the early and the late rains" (James 5:7). Life with God is weather dependent.

Third, agriculture involves *hard work*. When my father started his farm seven years ago, he was over 200 pounds. Now he is 160. Farming involves a lot of work. You must be creative, entrepreneurial, committed, and tough. There will be a lot of days where you find yourself doing things you would not like to be doing. A lot of days include some kind of stress because of an unforeseen problem. This is what life will be like with Jesus in his kingdom. It involves outside forces, yes, but also how those outside forces relate with our efforts, just like with a farmer. There will be a temptation to grumble, but with the hard work comes a reward one cannot experience anywhere else—one must be careful not to miss it (Matt. 20:1–16).

Fourth, agriculture *produces unique results*. Growing your own tomatoes instead of buying them at a supermarket will leave you with the greatest produce and the worst. Some of the tomatoes will taste better than any tomato you have ever tasted, but some will rot early on the vine. Everything you grow in your own garden will need to be thoroughly washed before you partake of it. You will have moments of great pride in the garden and great despair, contemplating the ways you could have tended differently to the produce. Within Jesus' great kingdom, results will vary (Matt. 13:8). Trusting the slow, hardworking process and relying on outside forces will give you a product that cannot be replaced by the manufactured and processed goods—you'll see something so much richer and truer: "the precious fruit of the earth" (James 5:7). But you will also see things die; things you planted and labored over will wash away. Jesus will be with you through each budding and dying fruit.

A Ministry of Participation and Pace

All of this talk about farmers and weather and fruit leads us to what Christians call "ministry." *Ministry is the process of partnering with God's work that benefits others.* It is not so much something we do, but rather, as Henri Nouwen says, "a process we trust."[13] If you look carefully at the definition, you'll notice *all Christians* participate in ministry. This is not only for religious professionals and clergy. My wife, a doctor, partners with God in the healing of children to their benefit. It is always God who heals, but her "ministry" is to partner with him in their healing. All Christians participate in ministry, where the active agent is God and the partner he chooses is his church, his people, us. But we are not the ones who manufacture this ministry; we are always the beneficiaries of it, even if we are the leaders of it. It's all grace.

In the twenty-first century, we miss Jesus' agricultural images for the images within our technologically advanced cities. Instead of speaking about the slow work of God, we talk about all we must accomplish "for him." Our focus becomes strategy instead of prayer, ambition instead of meditation, and vague platitudes instead of deep biblical wisdom. "Leadership" becomes more about running the organization than serving people the things they need.

13. Nouwen, "From Solitude to Community to Ministry."

We cannot abandon the soil for the microwave. Nothing about the ministry of Jesus would make us believe things go quickly with his work. Very often, his disciples were confused and frustrated by his slowness to react. Jesus had remarkable patience and pace, which would frustrate the Silicon Valley.

Many Christians I meet with aspire to "do great things for God," and many Americans make huge grabs for greatness. When we do this, we abandon the pace Jesus outlines for us. The world does not need many more "organizations"; the world needs patient people who commit themselves daily to the work God has right in front of them. We do not need any more amazing personalities; we need faithful believers who wake up each day and commit themselves to the small work of seed planting. This will often mean our big plans will be set aside in order to pray, and our careers will move more slowly because we have to be present with our neighbors. We'll have to share who Jesus is instead of waiting for our pastor to throw an outreach event. We must work at the pace of the taqueria, not of Facebook.[14]

Are we prepared to abandon the images of business and the city for the images of seeds and soil? Do our churches have the same marks as Jesus' agricultural parables? Are they slow, hardworking, dependent on the outside, and producing all kinds of unique results—both rotten and fresh? Ministry is not business. Pastors are not shopkeepers, as Eugene Peterson would say,[15] but are instead shepherds, tenders, and

14. Facebook's early motto was "Move Fast and Break Things." They have certainly done both.

15. Peterson, *Working the Angles*, 2. No one has written with more prophetic power on the integrity of pastoral ministry than Eugene Peterson. He is quite simply the greatest articulator of what it means to be a pastor. Reading him should be both challenging and refreshing to the twenty-first-century leader,

farmers. There is no such thing as an "executive" in ministry, because there is nothing to execute. Instead, we tend to the garden and beg for rain.

Where Is the End?

I've heard it said amongst short-distance runners that you can't be in serious competition to run the fastest 100 meters if you don't believe it can be run in zero seconds.[16] As the time for the fastest man on earth (100-meter dash) gets smaller and smaller, every runner in the competition believes themselves to be able to beat it . . . and beat it again. In other words, there is no number too small. They can always go faster.

The primary reason I question our American sensibility for fast growth in regards to ministry and Christian life is that there is no end. This is chasing the wind, is it not? The largest church in America is Joel Osteen's Lakewood Church, reporting over forty-three thousand attenders each Sunday. The largest church in the world is the Yoido Full Gospel Church in Seoul, South Korea, at nearly eight hundred thousand members. I suppose the Catholic Church has the "game" won; they have 1.2 billion members. The fastest-growing church in America in 2016 was Gateway Fellowship Church in San Antonio, Texas, growing at a rate of 187 percent in one year.[17]

---

and we would be fools to ignore this man's writing on the ministry. I could list off specific books, but everyone, especially those desiring to be clergy, would be served best by reading all of his work. William H. Willimon is a similar voice. For his perspective—an essential one for any pastor—see his simply titled book *Pastor*.

16. Malcolm Gladwell said this during an interview, and for the life of me I cannot remember where. But he said it. And he loves running. Carry on.

17. *Outreach*, "100 Fastest-Growing Churches in America 2016."

This is just church stuff. We can't even get into the statistics of growing businesses and schools and economies throughout the world. You get the picture. At the heart of all of this is this question: When will enough be enough for us? I know it is a simple question, but we have to understand that most churches will be small and many businesses will be too. And that doesn't mean they're "unsuccessful." Could it be that we sacrifice quality, capacity, joy, and peace when we serve the great, vague numbers in the sky leading us toward endless and unlimited growth? Maybe there's more truth in the taqueria. I sure hope so.

Isolation and Connection

Two can be as bad as one
It's the loneliest number since the number one
HARRY NILSSON, "One"

ix hundred years ago, no one moved. You lived where you were born, and, for the most part, you died there. No one traveled or went on vacation. You married someone near you and would never think it possible to escape your family once you were eighteen. Human societies existed in tribes and feudal systems anchored by village elders or, in the more advanced regions, a church parish. The only way toward a good life was through the people around you. You would not succeed—or fail, for that matter—apart from where you were born and who surrounded you. For tens of thousands of years, human life was limited by the community.

Throughout the 1500s and 1600s, an enormous movement of religious, philosophical, economic, and technological ideas burst forth and changed all of this. Everything from the Protestant Reformation to the printing press fundamentally altered our world, and while we received wonderful ideas and technologies through this era, we also inherited an individuality complex. Our technologies afforded us the ability to make a good life *for and by ourselves*. The changes in these centuries led to the Enlightenment, where empiricism, utilitarianism, and rationalism ultimately led us to what we call "individualism."

All of those "isms" aside, we are now, as a culture, convinced we do not need anyone to help us succeed. In a total reversal of human life, we now see other people as obstacles to our flourishing instead of aids. We now see the people around us as inhibiting us from achieving what we believe we have to do. The most celebrated individuals in our society are those who "did it by themselves" despite "the haters" or "the critics"—those who, *despite* their community, family, and place of birth, forged for themselves a new life of prosperity and success. The writer Richard Rodriguez observed, "Americans like to talk about the importance of family values, but America isn't a country of family values. . . . This is a country of people who leave home."[1]

A Good Motive?

In the previous chapter, I argued that our ambition to grow in every area of life is unsustainable and deadly. But what if

1. This is a summary of Rodriguez's thoughts by Krista Tippett, the host of the public radio program *On Being*. She said this when she interviewed him on her program in August of 2014, and he responded to her summary with an affirmative.

behind our ambition to grow was a good ambition to help more people? What if we wanted to grow our churches *in order to reach more people*? What if we wanted to grow our businesses *for the flourishing of society*? What if we wanted our economy to grow *so more people could enjoy life*? What if there were good reasons to grow?

Certainly many leaders assert this very premise, that growth is always good. It's what we've been told. Grow the church so more know Jesus. Scale a business so more can live better. Boost the economy so more people make more money. Beneath our love for bigger and better, for larger and more advanced, is, apparently, our love for humanity. Apparently.

So now we must ask the question: *Does growth lead to a better and more connected world?* Does the boosting of our economy, growth of churches, and upward mobility of our business plans lead us toward communities of love or of isolation? Is the narrative of American life—that bigger leads us toward something better—actually true? In such an advanced and wealthy time in history, shouldn't human communities be more connected than ever?

Unfortunately, it seems the vast research surrounding these questions points us to a negative answer. Instead of being more connected than ever, we're more isolated. In fact, it appears the very systems we used to reach such an advanced, wealthy age of civilization have cost us something. Our systems of capitalism, technology, philosophy—and even certain streams of theology—have given us more money than ever, but less connection, happiness, and fulfillment.

The Age of Hyper-Individualism

In the modern West, we are not simply individualists; we are "*hyper*-individualist."[2] Our economic and technological growth has come by way of further isolation. There is almost too much data to back up the fact that we work longer hours in greater isolation *because of* and *in service to* our own growth.

Our hyper-individualism has led us to utilize technology and mobility to succeed in spite of the people around us, and our social lives are disintegrating because of it. Our strides in how we get around (mobility) and how we communicate and get work done (through technology) have promised us a more connected, secure world. But this hasn't happened.

The average American has half as many close friends as those living fifty years ago.[3] Think about that. That's a massive change. In fact, more recent studies suggest Americans have, on average, just *two* close confidants.[4] Due to mobility and technology, Americans also replace half of their friend groups every seven years, which means if we only have five close friends, we're likely to carry only 2.5 of them for over a decade.[5] And if we have only two confidants, we'll be fortunate if just one of those relationships survives fifteen or twenty years.

Isolation and loneliness has been an increasing field of study in the past two decades, and the results are not uplifting.[6] Since 1980, the number of American adults who say

2. McKibben, *Deep Economy*, 96 (emphasis mine).
3. McKibben, "The Most Important Number in the World."
4. Stokes, "You Gotta Have Friends? Most Have Just 2 True Pals."
5. *Live Science* Staff, "Half of All Friends Replaced Every 7 Years."
6. A great short summary of this data was put together by Dr. Druhv Khullar in "How Social Isolation Is Killing Us."

they are lonely has doubled, from 20 percent to 40 percent.[7]
And among the elderly, those who lack social engagement
are more likely to die prematurely.[8]

This is a particularly American problem that gets worse
the richer we become.[9] I can remember first working in the
Tenderloin and realizing how connected the church community was with one another. While the neighborhood remained an isolating place, the church's networks of relationships were rather tight-knit. In our little inner-city church,
"community" was not a program we needed, because we
always saw each other all the time. No one had cars, few
owned a computer, and a lot of people spent their time walking around the one square mile of the neighborhood. Because
of this, relationships developed quickly, and when we didn't
see someone, we noticed. But when Americans make more
money, we build bigger houses farther away from each other.
We intentionally construct a kind of hyper-individualistic
life. It's called "the suburbs."

Perhaps the largest and most conclusive popular summary
of all of this data is Robert Putnam's landmark book *Bowling
Alone: The Collapse and Revival of the American Community*. Putnam, a political scientist at Harvard, pulled together
enormous amounts of data to show the absolute destruction of local communities, be they churches, schools, Boy
Scout troops, or neighborhood committees. He is convinced
that both modern mobility and technology have changed
American life forever.

7. *AARP The Magazine*, "Loneliness among Older Adults: A National Survey
of Adults 45+."
8. Holt-Lunstad, Smith, and Layton, "Social Relationships and Mortality
Risk."
9. Rosenblat, "The Wealthier You Get, the Less Social You Are."

Each day, we spend more time alone behind the wheel of a car (seventy-two minutes, on average) than cooking for our families (under thirty minutes), and any additional ten minutes of a commute cuts our community activities by an additional 10 percent.[10] How can we make it to our church small group or a PTA meeting if we're driving straight home to quickly make dinner before the kids go to bed?

In our mobile age, we do not consider how moving to a new city or spending endless months traveling for a new job might affect our lives. We believe it will make us happier if it includes "doing what we love." But doing what we love at the expense of being around those whom we love apparently wounds us more deeply than we're aware.

Technologized Community

In addition to mobility, technology has further distanced us from one another. Most of our workdays are spent in front of some sort of screen, and now our social life is on our devices as well. Connecting with old friends or meeting new ones happens through social structures that exist online, through profiles that present a constructed version of ourselves. We are not our profiles, but nearly everyone who meets us today meets "us" online first.

When a friend of mine was defending her presence on an online dating platform, she made a very solid, simple point: "What do you expect me to do?" she asked. "*This is where people are.*" It's strange, but we consider the location of people to be *online*. That's "where they are," even though

10. Putnam, *Bowling Alone*, 292–93.

there's no way to actually "be" online, because "online" is not a geographic, physical space. Nevertheless, that's where our community is: in our pocket, on a screen. The very location of people has shifted dramatically, and this has led us to spend our time differently.

Common in the Bay Area are "community work spaces" like WeWork, which should be called "isolated work spaces." While the sprawling and open physical layout would make you think these are community spaces where people exchange ideas, the opposite seems to be true. Every day, paying customers arrive with their laptops and headphones and work in front of a screen for the next eight hours, only stopping to talk to people when asked, "Is this seat taken?" Certainly technology offers much good, but we cannot ignore how it has fundamentally changed how we interact with one another. While promising a more connected world, the dramatic increase in mobility and technology has only further isolated us.

Maybe we could get personal for a second: How many of your neighbors know your name? And how many neighbors' names do you know? It recently struck me that, out of the dozens of people who live in my apartment building, I only know the names of maybe five. When I started to talk to my other friends who live in apartment buildings, the most common response I got was something like, "Dang, that's a lot!"

The answer is not a wholesale rejection of technology, but we need to take a closer look at how our world has changed for the worse in spite of all this ridiculous growth. But before we do that, we need to check our churches.

The Church of Self

Have the church and religious communities been as affected as the rest of the world in this new technological and mobile age?

The church has actually remained a bastion of hope in a community-less age. Statistics show people are happier if they're part of a small group that meets at least once a week, and those who attend religious services often have more friends.[11] Even more dramatically, if you join a small group that meets regularly for any reason—religious or not—it actually *halves* the chance that you will die within the next year.[12] There is certainly a place for the church in our age of increasing isolation. Again, we are talking quite literally about a life-or-death subject.

But is the church directing people toward community or toward hyper-individualism? Certainly this varies from church to church, but as Christians, we must be thinking about our faith as a localized community and not a group of isolated individuals.

When Jesus is asked, "What is the greatest commandment?" he responds with a *local and relational* command: "Love the Lord your God" and "Love your neighbor as yourself" (Matt. 22:36–40). When Jesus is asked to define what he means by "neighbor," he tells us about "the good Samaritan," a simple story about a man who encounters someone suffering along the road and helps him. In summary, your neighbor is the person near you (Luke 10:25–37). How much of Jesus' teachings involved a highly local life where we pay attention to those near us? Certainly we live in a different

11. Schwartz, "Tyranny of Choice."
12. New Economics Foundation, *Well-Being Manifesto*, 16 (quoted in McKibben, *Deep Economy*, 108).

world, but how many of us ignore this command because our theology is more about us than others?

As a pastor for over ten years, I cannot tell you how many times I hear the phrase "*my* faith" or "*my* relationship with God."[13] In modern American Christianity, our faith is *our own*. We are the ones who dictate it, and if you question it, we cry judgment and warn others by saying, "God knows *my* heart!" I'm afraid Karl Barth was right, even though he wrote nearly a century ago:

> Our relation to God is ungodly. We suppose that we know what we are saying when we say "God." . . . We allow ourselves an ordinary communication with him, we permit ourselves to reckon with him as though this were not extraordinary behavior on our part. We dare to deck ourselves out as his companions, patrons, advisers, and commissioners. . . .
>
> Secretly we are the masters in this relationship. We are not concerned with God, but with our own requirements, to which God must adjust himself. . . . Our well-regulated, pleasurable life longs for some hours of devotion, some prolongation into infinity. And so, when we set God upon the throne of the world, we mean by God ourselves. In "believing" on him, we justify, enjoy, and adore ourselves.[14]

How quickly does worshiping "God" sneakily become worshiping ourselves? My experience is that, without community, this is our default. Community cures us from the

---

13. Joseph H. Hellerman, a New Testament scholar quoted more in sections ahead, notes that the term "personal Savior" does not occur once in all of Scripture. Rather, the massive evidence from Paul and the other New Testament writers was on *our* Lord and *our* faith. See Hellerman, *When the Church Was a Family*, 7, 124–25.

14. Barth, *The Epistle to the Romans*, 44.

hyper-individualistic self-worship into which we so easily fall. Connection is the biblical way out of our isolated selves. If we read the statistics above correctly, we will see that involvement in a solid, local church—or any intentional community—has the potential to literally save someone's life.

The Gospel of Connection

In his remarkable study of "place" within Jewish and Christian thought, the Old Testament theologian Walter Brueggemann writes about its importance during a time when the "urban promise" has failed. "That promise," Brueggemann writes, "concerned human persons who could lead detached, unrooted lives of endless choice and no commitment. It was glamorized around the virtues of mobility and anonymity that seemed so full of promise for freedom and self-actualization. But it has failed. . . . It is now clear that a *sense of place* is a human hunger that the urban promise has not met. . . . It is *rootlessness* and not *meaninglessness* that characterizes the current crisis."[15]

If "rootlessness" truly is the characteristic of our modern crisis, then a compelling solution can and should be the *local* church—for the Christian *and* the non-Christian, ideally. It is in the local church that individuals get rooted in a place and connected to their neighbors. Community cures our innate desire to isolate ourselves in preservation of our ego. It is also here, in localized community under God's love, where individuals begin to hear and respond to the good news of the family found in Jesus Christ.

15. Brueggemann, *The Land*, 3–4.

The gospel message is the story of a God who exists in perfect, Triune community, and who, out of that community, pours his own love onto us. Through Christ, we are adopted as sons and daughters, brought into a connected family called the church. We become "the body of Christ," a metaphor explaining our close connection with God himself. The local church is simply the expression of the larger church the Triune God is connecting throughout the world. In a local church, we are reminded of two essential human facts: we are not alone and we do not exist for ourselves. These two truths liberate us from the deadly lie of isolation and remind us of our smallness while simultaneously teaching us about our kinship within such a large and complicated universe.

But this must be taught and practiced within our little or large congregations. As pastors, we are to reject "programitizing" the church into a bunch of routes where individuals' felt needs can be met. "God's intention," writes the New Testament scholar Joseph Hellerman, "is not to become the feel-good Father of a myriad of isolated individuals who appropriate the Christian faith as yet another avenue toward personal enlightenment."[16] Our work now is to fiercely and fully hold to the dominant metaphor of the early church: a family around a table.

The Work of Connection

The New Testament writers use various word pictures to capture the heart of the Christian *koinonia*, but none is used more than that of "brothers and sisters." Over and over again,

16. Hellerman, *When the Church Was a Family*, 7.

early Christians refer to each other as siblings, a part of the same family.

When seen in this way, it may appear too simple. Why isn't it working? In my understanding, although the gospel and the local church offer a simple cure for our lonely world, "simple" does not mean "easy."

Let me frame it by way of a dramatic example: when I was working in the inner city of San Francisco, my boss would always say that the root of homelessness in America was traumatic relationships. In other words, people became homeless for a variety of reasons, but ultimately their community structure fell apart: they had nowhere to go because they had no *one* to go to. At some point in their life, they made bad decisions or other people hurt them in major ways, and so they found themselves with no one who could help them. Homelessness would never happen to someone with a solid community and great relationships, but that's only because they had a privilege not everyone has: a connected and dedicated community of mercy.

To my boss, the problem of homelessness had a simple solution: *You. Us.* If the fundamental reason for homelessness is relational, then the solution is relational. If people began forging relationships with homeless people, homelessness would change. It's this simple *and* this difficult: if all of us decided homelessness was unjust, and just *some of us* decided to take one person into our homes only for the reason that we loved them and God loved them, there would be no homeless people.

We can do some math: there are (roughly) 6,500 homeless people in San Francisco right now. The city of San Francisco has (roughly) 865,000 people living in it. This means less than

1 percent of the population would have to step up in this major way—of loving his or her neighbor as themselves. We don't do this work because it's hard, and we'd much rather look for less-community-oriented solutions. We'd rather build housing of small apartments they can live in, or worse, buy them bus tickets to other cities so people we've never met in places we've never been can "deal with them."[17] In other words, we'd rather build a program than a relationship. San Francisco is already made up of around 9 percent Bible-believing Christians, so the numbers to stamp out homelessness are already there.[18] We just need the vision and commitment to make it so.

There are complications with this for sure, and I'm not suggesting this as the be-all and end-all solution for homelessness, but I am trying to expand our imagination about homelessness and even isolation in this world. Yes, some of my homeless friends enjoy being homeless, and certainly some of them do not want to stay with certain kinds of people in certain neighborhoods for all kinds of reasons. Mental illness and the immense effects of trauma in someone's life

17. This is a real solution to homelessness that has been happening for decades and, thanks to a recent investigation by the *Guardian*, has been shown to be ineffective. Read their exhaustive report on local American governments buying one-way bus tickets for homeless residents in their December 20, 2017, article "Bussed Out." San Francisco is one city of major focus in the report.

18. The number of Bible-believing Christians fluctuates a lot in San Francisco, because the city is highly transient. But the Pew Research Center reports this number in one of their recent surveys of major American cities and religious practices (Lipka, "Major U.S. Metropolitan Areas Differ in Their Religious Profiles"). One of the issues with studies such as this one is that they rely on what statisticians call "self-reporting." This means the studies rely on individuals declaring themselves "Bible-believing," which leads to numerous problems, as you can imagine. If someone says "I'm a Bible-believing Christian," then they are counted. There's nothing else to go by. That same person could be supporting unjust systems, cruel to their wife, and selfish with their spending. But if they say they're "Bible-believing," the statistician will count it.

complicate all of this. Nevertheless, has it ever occurred to you that you and I bear a kind of responsibility to the person sleeping outside every night? And are we aware of the incredible healing power of relationships? I have known many people whose entire physical appearance and future changed because they made a different friend.

It may seem overly dramatic, but is it wrong? There are countries and communities throughout history where we have no sign of significant numbers of homeless citizens. Why? Some cultures do not share our apathy toward homelessness.[19] Certain societies take serious responsibility for their neighbors through radical hospitality and lawmaking. *No one should be alone and no one should live on the street*, they think. We do not think that way. If we did, we would not have such horrific statistics of homelessness in America.

The church's work of obliterating isolation goes beyond those who have no homes, because this issue is not exclusive to those living in a tent under a bridge. There are so many lonely people in our world that the British government recently installed a "Minister for Loneliness," citing data that over "nine million people . . . often or always feel lonely."[20] Our neighbors are lonely, whether they have a home or not, and

19. Japan, in particular, is an interesting case study in lowering homelessness in a highly populated country. For a decent summary of the story of Japan and homelessness in the twenty-first century (particularly in Tokyo), see Hongo, "Homelessness in Tokyo Hits Record Low." Finland provides another example. See Foster, "What Can the UK Learn."

20. See the Jo Cox Commission on Loneliness: https://www.jocoxloneliness .org. UK prime minister Teresa May said, "I want to confront this challenge for our society and for all of us to take action to address the loneliness endured by the elderly, by careers, by those who have lost loved ones—people who have no one to talk to or share their thoughts and experiences with." A full report in the *New York Times* offers further insights: Yeginsu, "U.K. Appoints a Minister for Loneliness."

loneliness can lead to terrible decisions and life-threatening situations. The best thing to offer our neighbors—whether homeless or just lonely—is *us*. But how can we offer "us"?

The Power of the Table

In October 2016, during the most tumultuous and contentious election cycle in recent memory, the *New York Times* columnist David Brooks visited David Simpson and Kathy Fletcher, a couple who host a weekly meal for fifteen to twenty low-income kids in the Washington, DC, area. It all started when their son, Santi, told them about a friend at his school who was hungry and had no place to eat some nights. His friend was from a low-income family struggling to get by, a situation all too common in the DC area. One friend for dinner quickly turned into fifteen, and now the couple hosts a weekly meal with a few rules: hug everyone, eat as much as you like, share something no one here knows about you, perform something if you like, and no cell phones.

Brooks went to Thursday night meals for two years (and, as far as I know, still attends them) and reflected on his experience: "Poverty up close is so much more intricate and unpredictable than the picture of poverty you get from the grand national debates. The kids can project total self-confidence one minute and then slide into utter lostness the next." Brooks became deeply affected not by a policy or an idea but by a connection. Throughout the piece, you can hear that his heart has been changed by the relationships he has made with the kids he met.

"Souls are not saved in bundles," he concludes. "Love is the necessary force. The problems facing this country are deeper than the labor participation rate and ISIS. *It's a crisis of solidarity*, a crisis of segmentation, spiritual degradation and intimacy."[21]

This is the report of one couple packing their dinner table with intimacy and connection each Thursday night. Could Christians in the twenty-first century live a kind of rebellious life against hyper-individualism by offering environments of connection in an increasingly isolated world? It's amazing what a table can do. There is no program for a weekly meal, no large vision or organizational structure or business plan. But you can see what this meal did for this columnist—something no technology, philosophy, or economy can do—it changed his heart.

We can see now the need for such friendship on both ends of the socioeconomic spectrum. Those who are without a house, sleeping on the street, need relationships with those who are vastly different from them, and the opposite is true: those in the penthouse apartments on Fifth Avenue in New York City or Nob Hill in San Francisco need the transformative experience of being friends with someone who cannot afford running water. The rich need the poor and the poor need the rich. Connection can cure all kinds of personal dysfunction that comes from having tons of money or from not having enough.

Table Fellowship

The local church can offer the remarkably simple and healing practice of the table fellowship as a counter-narrative

21. Brooks, "The Power of a Dinner Table" (emphasis mine).

to the American Story of individualism. The local church is the collected number of Jesus followers in a particular area, who gather around common vision and creed. This means our response to the isolation in our country is both collective and individual. We will brainstorm, serve, and counteract isolation together, but we will also bear the responsibility with our individual resources. The local church is me *and* you—which, when put together, is "we." Together, as the church, we will open our tables for fellowship.

Table fellowship is the ancient Christian discipline of eating together. It's really that simple. In the early church, during the years AD 60–300, there was a common practice of sharing a meal together, what became known as the "agape feast" or the "love feast." These were potlucks of epic proportions where Christians would host believers and non-believers in their homes for a long meal. They most certainly took this from Jesus, who was no stranger to a good meal with friends. Every Gospel account makes several mentions of Jesus sitting at a table with all kinds of different people, which seems to emphasize his deep commitment to table fellowship (Matt. 9:10; 26:7, 20; Mark 2:15; 16:14; Luke 7:37; 11:37; 22:14; John 12:2; 13:23). This is how we, as the church, offer ourselves to a lonely world.

In American Christianity, one is "saved" in a personal, individualized sense. But as Hellerman argues, the Bible presents salvation as "a community-creating event."[22] He calls this the "familification" of the Christian, which happens simultaneously alongside the "justification" of the individual. One is not saved into isolated spirituality, but into a family

22. Hellerman, *When the Church Was a Family*, 120–43.

with brothers and sisters around a table—and that table is wide open. It is at the table—what Bonhoeffer called "life together"—that we enact all the various functions of a family: we share our possessions, our hearts, and our pain, and we elevate the needs of others above our own.

The biblical counter-narrative to an age of isolation is not a fresh program or a differing technology—it's not even the maximization of existing technologies and structures. The Bible meets an increasingly isolated world with a table. The battle is not won in better community programs or "small-group initiatives," but rather in ordinary Christians hosting meals for their neighbors on a regular basis, or believers staying in the communities people usually leave. Of course, table fellowship can happen *within* such "initiatives" and programs, but these things are not required. It looks like a lasting *rootedness*, a connection to a particular place with a particular people. I love what the writer Andy Crouch has said: "Our mission is not primarily to 'engage the culture' but to 'love our neighbor.' Our neighbor is not an abstract collective noun, but a real person in a real place."[23] Beware of a broad, theoretical theology without any names and faces. Beware of life without a table.

A Journey Home

For a year and a half, I was commuting long hours to my work in the inner city of San Francisco. My wife and I lived in the Silicon Valley, where she works, but a dream job in the Tenderloin opened up and I had to take it. I loved being close

23. Crouch, "Stop Engaging 'The Culture.'"

to the poor and working alongside an organization committing itself to a particular people in a particular place. I was
so fortunate to be hired on their staff. The only problem was
the commute: it was brutal. In typical Bay Area fashion, I
used my car, a train ride, and a long walk to total an hour-
and-a-half trip to work—three hours total every day.

The commute afforded me a lot of time to think, pray,
read, and listen to podcasts. I think I became more reflective
during that time, which is a good thing. And it was during
those long commutes that I began to think a lot about my
neighbors, and more accurately, how I didn't know them.
My wife and I started reading news reports and listening to
our community more and realized there was so much work
to do closer to where we lived. I was ignoring our neighborhood to go work in another. My wife was working six miles
from our apartment, but our ministry (where I worked and
our church family) was an hour or more away. Something
needed to change.

That's when we formed a little Bible study with people in
our neighborhood. Our Tuesday night group has become a
beautiful representation of table fellowship, our little rebel-
lion against the American narrative of hyper-individualism.
Each week, my wife and I walk from our apartment around
the corner to Colin and Jen's house, where about eight of us
sit together to talk about Scripture and pray for one another.
Every month, we party—food, drink, and often a game or a
movie—in order to experience what the Bible commands of
us: to love our neighbors. In spite of the Silicon Valley's cry for
isolated success, we have chosen to connect with those nearby.

I ended up stepping down from the dream job in the city.
When I read the Scriptures, I realize the work before me is

quite literally *before me*. And even if it means being a little smaller with a different job title, I better take it because it is in God's will, as described in what he calls the "greatest commandment" (Matt. 22:38 NLT). It's very hard to love people you live far away from. Well, maybe better put: it's easier to pretend to love people when you live far from them.

So, my wife and I committed to some smaller work closer to where we live here in the Silicon Valley. Certainly we still commute, and yes, in this day and age, it's impossible to walk everywhere for everything all the time. But it is possible to have people over for dinner, something we're doing with much greater regularity now. And it is possible to get to know the people around us. Table fellowship is something all of us can experience.

How are we to act in spite of increasing isolation? We call our neighbors. We invite people over. We know the names of the people we work with and become interested in their lives. We talk to people at our churches and visit people in prison. There is no program for this, but there is the community of Jesus—the church—which is perfectly set up for this. It's this simple, and it's this difficult. Jesus told us a truly abundant and rich life comes through a "narrow" path—difficult, but clear. Committing ourselves to the family of God through table fellowship in an increasingly isolated age is just that.

The hidden blessing of surrounding ourselves with an unlikely community through table fellowship is that it forces our attention off of ourselves. This becomes increasingly essential, especially when the American Story is telling you its favorite lie: *it's all about you*.

Fame and Obscurity

The occupational hazard of making a spectacle of yourself, over the long haul, is that at some point you buy a ticket too.

THOMAS MCGUANE, *Panama*

You're invisible now, you got no secrets to conceal.

BOB DYLAN, "Like a Rolling Stone"

There's this fascinating scene I keep thinking about from the *Frontline* documentary "Generation Like," where the host Douglas Rushkoff is sitting with a small group of millennials, asking them about their relationship with technology and media. It's a great conversation. Among other things, the documentary uncovers this generation's unique association with fame. No longer do young people desire to be famous—they *expect* to be famous: "It's not, 'Is he on TV, is he an actor, is he a good skateboarder?' It's 'famous.' That's

[the] word."[1] It doesn't matter what people do or how good they are at something; it matters if they're a celebrity.

But in this particular scene, Rushkoff asks the kids he's sitting with to define "selling out." They can't. And why do they have trouble defining such a simple cultural term? Because they don't even know what it means to "sell out."

This is where I realize I'm sort of on the edge of being a millennial. I don't identify with this scene at all. Not only do I know what it means to "sell out," but I grew up keenly aware of it and often consider this when making career decisions—and I'm a pastor. Nevertheless, it's clear that for my generation as a whole, "selling out" is not a concern anymore. The goal of most startups in the Silicon Valley is *precisely* to "sell out"—to Google.

"Generation Like" colors the data behind the millennial generation. But the data is, as always, incomplete. The desire to be famous isn't solely a millennial problem; it's a human problem. Millennials didn't appear from outer space, we were formed and nurtured in homes and families with real moms and dads, or lack thereof. No generation appears into the world from a clean, untouched background. Trends among a particular generation do not reveal uniqueness to them alone, but something common to all of us. The desire to be famous is just a human wish my generation is leading all of us in discovering.

Known and Celebrated

Fame is the natural consequence of a world of isolated hyper-individualists. As I discussed in the previous chapter,

1. PBS, "Generation Like."

the narrative of American life and the culture of growth has led us toward less connected, remote lives as swollen individualists. And so what happens next in our American narrative? In short, we isolate ourselves in order to (or as we) build ourselves up—to make our name great. We want everyone to know us for something we did or someone we have become.

When I use the word "fame," there are probably many of you who would not identify with this. You hate the spotlight. You despise attention. When you're asked to say something in front of a group, you're paralyzed. You hate having your picture taken. Becoming famous is your nightmare. And you can easily excuse yourself out of this chapter and this part of the story. But let's understand this term more deeply, not as a term of celebrity, but as a term of humanity.

Fame is *the condition of being known and celebrated by many people based on what we have done.* With this broad definition, each of us, when honest, should be able to locate ourselves within it.

Think about your job. Isn't one of the worst things to have happen at work doing something honorable for the company and having no one recognize you for it? When we put in all the work and get zero recognition, we see it as an injustice. Or think about your family. As a youth pastor for over ten years, I can attest to the vast amount of damage that can be done to a human being when their father or mother never recognizes anything they do. Constant criticism or even just ambivalence toward our accomplishments leads us into despair. We want to be known and we want to be celebrated—that is a key part of being a human, and we Americans have acquiesced to this desire.

During an interview with *Rolling Stone* in 1987, the writer Tom Wolfe claimed "youth culture" as the most significant trend to come from the West in the 1960s. More than the civil rights movement or Vietnam, Wolfe says, there's no match for what young people did across every major movement in the '60s. It was the young generation that brought about the various "movements" of the mid-century period: civil rights, the sexual revolution, the women's movement, anti-war protests, rock and roll, and so on. "And they did it because they had money. For the first time . . . young people had the *money*, the *personal freedom* and the *free time* to build monuments and pleasure palaces to their own tastes."[2]

These "monuments and pleasure palaces" started as institutions like Woodstock and *Playboy* magazine, but they evolved to become individuals: pop stars, entertainers, and athletes became our economy and objects of worship. Names and faces, people with Social Security numbers, became empires and memorials in their own right. As a culture, we moved from pleasure-feeding institutions to pleasure-feeding individuals. And we'll pay for both.

The cultural critic Chuck Klosterman writes this about Britney Spears: "Every day, random people use Britney's existence as currency; they talk about her public failures and her lack of talent as a way to fill the emptiness of their own normalcy. . . . [Celebrities] allow Americans to understand who they are and who they are not; they allow Americans to unilaterally agree on something they never need to consciously consider. A person like Britney Spears surrenders her

---

2. Wolfe, "Tom Wolfe on How to Write New Journalism" (emphasis mine).

privacy and her integrity and the rights to her own persona, and in exchange we give her huge sums of money."[3]

In the twenty-first-century Twitter era, we've gone a step further: now, these "monuments and pleasure palaces" are no longer cultural institutions like *Rolling Stone*, Studio 54, or Wall Street (certainly what Wolfe was alluding to), and they're also no longer individuals like Britney Spears or Justin Bieber. Instead, these monuments are something altogether more interesting and intimate: they're *us*.

What have we done with everything we've been given? We've constructed monuments of ourselves: profiles and personal websites and feeds that are all about us, serve us, and (in our minds) glorify us. The internet is a never-ending echo chamber of our own preconceived notions about the world, filled with advertisements based on our search history and clicks, right next to a feed forged from an algorithm that has a PhD in our personal online behavior. Online, the world actually *does* revolve around us. Our phones and technology do not serve us, they worship us.

The Lure and Centrality of Fame

When I was starting my writing career, I spent some time consulting with my friends who had been published before me. My buddy Paul makes a living with words, as an author and an editor.[4] I remember visiting him at his home in the woods of Oregon one day, showing him the proposal for my first book, *Distant God*. We were on a walk when he told me

3. Klosterman, *Eating the Dinosaur*, 73–74.
4. Paul is the best editor with whom I've ever worked (other than the editors of this book, of course). Find out more about him here: http://www.pauljpastor.com.

about what I have heard from many others since: the "three C's of publishing."[5] These concepts exist as a kind of folklore in the publishing world, and Paul was simply passing along what he had heard and learned from others in the business.

"First, you need a Concept. This is the idea of your book," Paul explained. "If anyone is going to publish you, the concept of your book needs to be compelling, hitting at a felt need in the current culture." This made sense to me. No one will be interested in publishing a book about a bad idea.

Second is the Craft, Paul explained. You just need to be a great writer. You need to know the elementary functions of language (a rarity in today's world), and you need to employ them with creativity. Your voice must be developed, and you need to be able to demonstrate a level of competency regarding vocabulary.

But finally—and, unfortunately in the publishing world, most importantly—you need the Crowd. How many people know you? How many people like you? How many people celebrate your ideas and could champion your book? All of my writing career, I've been told I lack this, and there are many authors who lack the first two C's but have a huge Crowd. They get publishing deals. I've had to rely on the first two.

The publishing world is no different from the rest of the world. If people love you, your life is much, much easier. If a crowd consistently follows you and applauds you, there will be certain obstacles and realities you will not have to con-

5. For the life of me I cannot find out who coined these terms. Paul Pastor is certainly is not the author of these concepts, and too many people on the internet try to take credit for this. I would warn you not to Google it if, like me, you're repulsed by platform-building pseudo gurus. This is not the "Three C's of Hiring," which are Character, Competency, and Chemistry. Enough reading in the business literature section would lead you to believe they have a unique affinity for the letter.

front. This is why we seek fame—or at least why we wouldn't mind having it. We seem to be certain that a lot of our current problems would change or go away if more people knew us and celebrated our work.

Throughout my career, many people have pointed me toward resources to help "grow my platform." This is a whole subindustry of business writing and coaching. Some people have built a platform on how to build a platform. These "techniques" involve harnessing social media, developing "fresh content," and "clarifying your message." Most of it is useless, and all of it is self-indulgent, but it's where we have been led naturally by technology.

Everything above comes from my personal experience—and I'm a pastor. I am surrounded by a surprising number of "examples" of what it means to be a pastor who have nothing to do with the biblical description of a spiritual leader. It's difficult to not be discouraged by the amount of white-teethed pastors on HD screens who sloppily exegete Scripture in the name of hype for a crowd. Like watching cheerleaders for a team I dislike in a sport I don't understand, I am often left bewildered. If I see another social media profile of a pastor who has labeled himself a "thought leader" or a "culture shaper," I actually might barf. Many of these men and women are the kinds of people I should probably get to know if I want to sell more books, but I can't help but think I have nearly nothing in common with them.

The life-sucking pull of celebrating yourself is not only inescapable, it's unfulfilling. In the novel *Infinite Jest*, about a quarter of the way through the book there's a scene set inside a sauna, where two semipro tennis players, LaMont Chu and Lyle, discuss the allure of tennis stardom. Chu desires to have his picture in magazines, to have his name said on television. He has a "rabid ambition" driving him toward becoming great and having people recognize him for it ("I guess it would give my life some sort of kind of meaning," he says at one point). Lyle is a sort of sage among the tennis club, and the two of them get into a philosophical discussion on the human appetite for celebrity.

In the discussion, Lyle says, "After the first photograph has been in a magazine, the famous men do not *enjoy* their photographs in magazines so much as they fear that their photographs will cease to appear in magazines. They are trapped, just as you are. . . . To be envied, admired, is not a feeling. Nor is fame a feeling. There are feelings associated with fame, but few of them are any more enjoyable than the feelings associated with envy of fame. . . . What fire dies when you feed it?"[6]

6. Wallace, *Infinite Jest*, 389. It is all the more fascinating reading this section in light of Wallace's life *after* this book was published. Before *Infinite Jest*, Wallace was known, but not a literary celebrity. *Infinite Jest* launched him to become a "voice of a generation" kind of writer, something Wallace struggled with deeply. In an interview with Charlie Rose in 1997, just one year after *Infinite Jest* was published, he talks about getting too much attention too quickly at too young of an age. Wallace seemed to want nothing more than to be a famous writer when he was younger, but then when he got famous, he became deeply depressed and suicidal. Wallace ultimately took his own life. He was found hanging in his garage with the near-finished manuscript of his long-awaited novel, *The Pale King*, sitting on his desk, the light from outside shining directly on it in a sort-of-supernatural way (Max, "Rereading David Foster Wallace"). His relationship with fame was like a combination of Lyle's and LaMont Chu's: deeply envious of those who had it, but massively uncomfortable with it once he obtained it. This was more deeply explored in the movie *The End of the Tour*, which traces the tail end of Wallace's first massive book tour and is based on the book *Every Love Story Is a Ghost Story: A Life of David Foster Wallace* by D. T. Max. In the movie, Wallace is played by Jason Segel, and I still can't decide if I like it or not. Nevertheless, reading this section of *Infinite Jest* in light of Wallace's own struggle with fame is not only the subject of the movie, but probably the subject of many boring dissertations on postmodern literature.

Lyle goes on to talk about how desire for attention—the "envy of fame"—might feel like being trapped in a cage, but once you get the fame, you're still trapped in the cage, just with a different kind of fear and envy: envy of those who lead normal lives and a fear that the attention will go away one day. You're just trading fears: "Do not believe the photographs," Lyle says. "Fame is not the exit from the cage."[7]

We believe that if people would just notice us, our lives would be easier and happier. If our bosses would recognize us for the work we've done, and if we would receive some kind of attention, we think there would be a kind of freedom associated with it, but that isn't the case. Some of the most imprisoned people we know are the celebrities we follow. They have to be what we want them to be, nothing less and nothing more.

But this also should not be of much surprise to me, even though it is, because from what I see in Scripture, this is all a part of our sin-infected DNA. Desiring to be known and celebrated for who we are and what we do is by no means a twenty-first-century problem.

Two Lies of Pride

Technological advances aside, the main biblical stories tell of the same core temptations of fame. The promise of the serpent (the mysterious, deceitful tempter in the story) to the man and woman is that by eating the fruit, they will "be like God." As Old Testament scholar John Sailhamer notes, the first couple chose to be *like* God instead of *with* him.[8]

7. Wallace, *Infinite Jest*, 389.
8. Sailhamer, *The NIV Compact Bible Commentary*, 18.

And we do the same today. The first big lie our ego tells us to justify our pride is that *we can be like God.*

The second lie is that we absolutely must *make a name for ourselves.* Just eight chapters after the story of the fall, the writer of Genesis tells the story of the tower of Babel, whose construction managers and leaders make the vision of their project to "make a name for ourselves" (Gen. 11:4). The project of the ancient society seems to be the same as that of the 1960s and '70s as outlined by Tom Wolfe above. A fresh reading of these early Jewish and Christian stories will humble us away from any accolades regarding our "progress." Not much has changed here either.[9]

These two banner messages—to be like God and to make a name for ourselves—run throughout the story of Scripture. Permeating the Old Testament are stories of kings, priests, prophets, husbands and wives, family members, and business owners buying into these two messages. Jacob and Esau fight over their birthright, the people of Israel make idols and grumble, Saul is envious of David's early success—all of these share the same roots of either desiring to be just

---

9. This makes me think of a fantastic aside in Andrew Delbanco's history of American higher education. He writes about first reading *The Iliad* as a freshman at Columbia, when his class had an astonishing realization together. They had read a scene in which Homer uses a metaphor of destruction, comparing it to little boys making sandcastles only to knock them down, "when we suddenly felt as if we were reading about ourselves—or at least, if we were male—our childhood selves. . . . Apparently, little boys on the shores of the Aegean three thousand years ago did the same thing that little boys do today at Jones Beach or the Hamptons. Whatever the explanation for such transhistorical truths, certain books—old and not so old—speak to us in a subversive whisper that makes us wonder whether the idea of progress might be a sham" (Delbanco, *College*, 101). I don't think I've ever read something more true about why young people must read old books. For all we might say about our "progress" technologically, economically, and so on, there are more true things that mostly stay the same for thousands of years. At some level, progress is an illusion.

like God or hoping to make a name. These two temptations become the infected root from which the tree of pride grows. Fame and celebrity is just a foreseeable outcome of such sin.

Seen through this theological lens, we can understand our modern age as just another version of the same story. Again, nothing much has changed. Our habits and goals revolve around being something like a god—renowned in the world and worshiped by others. We want to "make a name for ourselves." We lust after a byline, we seek credit for a job done, and we build our profiles to be "liked" by others. What is the Bible's counter-narrative to such a selfish story?

Hidden

To begin to see the Christian's vision for life in an age of celebrity, we need to return (again) to Jesus' metaphors for life with God or life in "the kingdom," as he called it. God's kingdom is "the range of God's effective will," the space over which God rules and reigns.[10] The kingdom is those places in life where God is in charge and the things he desires are happening and growing.

In order to capture the vast creativity of "God's kingdom," Jesus used word pictures and parables. In chapter 4 I mentioned that most of these metaphors were agricultural, telling us about the slow and passive nature of "growth" in

10. This definition is mostly borrowed from Dallas Willard. The website Soul Shepherding offers all of Willard's small, one-sentence definitions. Especially in his Christian writings, Willard is famous for taking highly complex theological topics and defining them with short sentences (e.g., his definition for beauty is "God's goodness made manifest to the senses"). His exact words for "the kingdom of heaven" are "the range of God's effective will." The webpage is helpful and thought-provoking: http://www.soulshepherding.org/2013/05/dallas-willards-definitions/.

our life with God. But Jesus' metaphors did not have just one common thread.

Here are some of the things Jesus likens to the kingdom of God: leaven, treasure, seeds, and pearls. All of these are mentioned multiple times in the Gospel accounts of Jesus' life and teaching. They also have one thing in common: they're all hidden.

Jesus tells us life with God is like leaven, which one puts in bread dough, causing it to change its flavor and shape entirely (Matt. 13:33). Or it's like a treasure hidden in a field, where one must dig it up from under the ground in which it's buried (Matt. 13:44). Or the kingdom is like a mustard seed, the smallest of all seeds, and yet, when planted underneath the surface, it grows into a large tree providing a home to the birds (Mark 4:30–32). Or life with God is likened to a pearl, which is discovered only under the sea within the confines of a shell (Matt. 13:45–46). To Jesus, life with God begins in a hidden place, in obscurity. Perhaps our pursuit of being known and acknowledged moves us further away from God's activity.

More Intimately Part of the World

Pierre Teilhard de Chardin was a Jesuit priest, an idealist philosopher, and a scientist specializing in geology and paleontology. He spent most of his life working to reconcile religion and scientific theory. In his personal (and highly theological) reflections on studying science, and particularly studying fossils and the earth, de Chardin wrote, "I discovered that there could be a deep satisfaction in working in obscurity—like leaven, or a microbe. In some way, it seems to me you become more intimately a part of the world."[11]

Could it be that in our glorification and oversharing of our lives, we have lost a kind of joy found only in a life of obscurity? Jesus calls us to be, as de Chardin puts it, "intimately part of the world." We are to love our neighbors, care for the poor, share what we have with each other, and pray for the people in our lives who trouble us. How can we do such things if we are obsessed with "making it"?

The entire concept of spiritual growth is, scripturally speaking, "a biological/agricultural metaphor dealing with timing and passivity, not a mathematical metaphor dealing with accumulation and multiplication."[12] For a Christian to grow in the twenty-first century, he or she must hide themselves in a life with God.

This, of course, can be taken all sorts of ways. Does this mean Christians should become monastic in their religious practice, selling everything to hide away in the foothills to pray and meditate, without any interaction with "the world"? Absolutely not—look again at the metaphors of Jesus.[13]

11. Quoted in Peterson, *Under the Unpredictable Plant*, 137.

12. Peterson, *Under the Unpredictable Plant*, 138.

13. Perhaps more should be said here, and said more specifically in response to Rod Dreher's highly debated book *The Benedict Option*, which David Brooks said was "the most discussed and most important religious book of the decade" ("The Benedict Option"). I hesitate to disagree with an intellectual force like Brooks, yet I will. Rob Bell's *Love Wins* was released in 2011, and while both men ended up being profiled in the *New Yorker* and both books warranted "response" books of their own, *Love Wins* was talked about more broadly outside of intellectual circles. Maybe I can put it this way: high school kids were asking me about *Love Wins*; they had no idea what *The Benedict Option* was. The noise surrounding the books aside, *The Benedict Option* had many flaws outlined best by other reviewers. Nevertheless, I'm grateful for the conversation Dreher started regarding our collective role in society as Christians in the modern age. It's just a bit too prescriptive, and the prescriptions don't help the disease. It also doesn't help that

The kingdom of God is often found hidden *within* an environment, not excavated *out of* an environment or seen in plain sight. The leaven is *within* the bread, the seed is planted *in* the soil, the treasure is *buried in* the ground, and so on. All of these things are in direct contact and even partnership with the elements surrounding them. The kingdom of God is discovered and seen first from inside the hidden, sullied places. Spirituality is not sterile; it is filthy. Jesus seemed to be careful to help us understand that while we will live with God in plain sight, we will not always see what he is up to there. We will be, like leaven or a microbe, hidden with God in plain sight.

This might help us understand Jesus' teachings about generosity, prayer, and fasting. In all three of these teachings, delivered back-to-back-to-back in his famous Sermon on the Mount, Jesus repeats this phrase three times: "Your Father

---

Dreher later wrote derogatory remarks after President Trump allegedly called nations like Haiti "s**thole countries." In his blog, Dreher said, "Let's think about Section 8 housing. If word got out that the government was planning to build a housing project for the poor in your neighborhood, how would you feel about it? Be honest with yourself. Nobody would consider this good news. You wouldn't consider it good news because you don't want the destructive culture of the poor imported into your neighborhood. Drive over to the poor part of town, and see what a s**thole it is. Do you want the people who turned their neighborhood [into] a s**thole to bring the s**thole to your street? No, you don't. Be honest, you don't" (Dreher, "Of Sh*tholes and Second Thoughts"). Actually, yes, I do. Christians should gravitate *toward* the poor, not away from them, and our proximity to them demonstrates our proximity to Christ. When the poor are close to us, we are close to Jesus. Therefore, it is *precisely* good news if a Christian hears of Section 8 housing going in right next to us. One cannot divorce Dreher's opinion expressed here with what he calls "the Benedict Option." Now, reading the book in full context, we can see it for what it is: Christians abdicating themselves from the mess of earthly life. Dreher, we can see now, wishes for his own Christian utopia, away from Section 8 housing and nonbelieving people in deep poverty. He wants clean Christianity, away from the mess. I do not. I think we're called not *from* the mess, but to it. This, put with my comments above regarding the agricultural and hidden nature of Jesus' metaphors, should help Christians pause when hearing arguments for "the Benedict Option" and things like it.

who sees in secret will reward you" (Matt. 6:4, 6, 18). He
tells his followers to give money without blasting trumpets
about it, to pray behind a closed door, and to look healthy
and not feeble when fasting. All of these teachings are given
to persuade us that the true joy (or "reward") of following
God is not in fame but obscurity. We will be most connected
to God, his life, and his people when we act in such a way.
Hidden in plain sight.

Fullness

I'm not sure there is a better way to close this chapter than by
retelling the story of Henri Nouwen. Nouwen was a Catholic priest and theologian who reached the highest place of
theological academia. For ten years, Nouwen was a professor
of theology at Yale Divinity School, and before that was a
visiting professor at Notre Dame. He had the highest kind
of success and fame one can achieve in Catholic theology.

During his time at Yale, Nouwen visited a small community caring for the disabled called Daybreak. There, Nouwen's vocation was transformed. He found the true community of Christ hidden in plain sight. In a world of ivy-covered
towers and world-renowned books, he had missed Jesus. But
when he met with the poor and disabled, he found God all
over again, years after his ordination. Nouwen resigned from
his professorship and spent the last ten years of his ministry
among the disabled, serving as their pastor.

Nouwen's reflections on leadership in the modern world
were published in 1989 under the title *In the Name of Jesus*.
In the book, he urges pastors of the twentieth century to
move "from relevance to prayer" and "from popularity to

ministry." He saw in both the careers of laypeople and the trajectory of religious leaders in America "a deep current of despair" running underneath all of the fame and success. Things looked good on the surface, but we were rotting underneath. "While efficiency and control are the great aspirations of our society," Nouwen wrote, "the . . . feelings of emptiness and depression, and a deep sense of uselessness fill the hearts of millions of people in our success-oriented world."[14] Nouwen's great realization was that there was much more of God's activity among a tiny community of disabled people than in the high halls of academia.

Nouwen's story reminds me of the biblical book of Ruth. Sandwiched in between the Old Testament's most violent and chaotic books, Ruth is the story of an immigrant widow who finds a surprising spouse and lives happily ever after. Just four chapters long, the story takes place away from the hustle of Israel's political turmoil and the centers of their government, which was, at the time, in shambles. The book is set on a farm and stars characters we've not heard of, until the end, when we realize the story is about the parents of a man named Obed, who was the father of Jesse, who was the father of King David. Not until the end of the story do we realize the book's profound message: while violence and corruption haunt the "center" of Israel's life, out on the margins God is furthering his redemptive purposes with an immigrant widow and her new husband. God's work—his ministry—is often hidden in plain sight.

Doing ministry and living our life "in the name of Jesus" will mean finding him in the hidden places, where no fa-

14. Nouwen, *In the Name of Jesus*, 20–21.

mous or powerful person lives. We will find God in places social media cannot reinterpret to look cool and slick, and in the spaces no politician would visit and no television show would highlight. We will find God in positions that don't build our résumé and might actually make it look worse. And we should expect to see God in those the culture finds no value in: the landscapers, the elderly, the mentally unstable, the stay-at-home dads, the simple, the homeless, the broke, those in debt, the waiters and waitresses, the janitors, the single moms, the criminals, and even our little children. God is with such people our culture has deemed unremarkable.

Our great hope then, as those living out the Bible's counter-narrative, is that God *is* present and at work in our world. If we take Jesus at his word, that life in him is found in hidden places like leaven and seed, then we need not fret when what we see in plain sight is disastrous. It certainly is unsettling to see our current political moment, to read the news and scan our social media feeds. But as Christians we know the great secret of the universe: that what happens in plain sight is not all that's happening. God might be more active in the homeless encampment than the White House. He certainly was telling us something when Jesus was born in a stable far away from any royal courts.

There's always something beneath the surface that is much more important and powerful. God's kingdom—his powerful activity on the earth—will not be plain to see, but if one has the "ears to hear" or the "eyes to see," as Jesus himself said, they will never live in the world the same way again. As we grow in Christ, we will constantly find ourselves obeying God in secret, obscure places, because we will know what Jesus knew: that's where the action is.

"The great message that we have to carry," Henri Nouwen wrote, "is that God loves us not because of what we do or accomplish, but because God has created and redeemed us in love and has chosen us to proclaim that love as the true source of all human life."[15] So long as we seek fame and celebrity, we will focus on our accomplishments, but so long as we know Christ's power and love, we will look for him where he told us to: beneath the surface, hidden in plain sight.

Nevertheless, it will remain difficult to shed our desire to be celebrated, mainly because being celebrated gives us something our heart longs for: power.

15. Nouwen, *In the Name of Jesus*, 17.

Power and Vulnerability

There are three aspects of nature which command man's
attention: power, loveliness, grandeur. Power he exploits,
loveliness he enjoys, grandeur fills him with awe.

ABRAHAM JOSHUA HESCHEL, *Man Is Not Alone*

In the fall of 2017, a massive and important conversation
around sexual assault in America began. Sparked by
the allegations against the Hollywood producer Harvey
Weinstein, the #MeToo movement (as it has been called in
sum) caught fire through nearly all forms of media and lit
ablaze the careers of countless men in the entertainment
business. Nearly every day, a new accusation came against
another man, and another career was laid ashen.

The #MeToo movement is more like a forest fire than a
house fire: its damage is a kind of clearing out, an expos-
ing of injustices that lay dormant for years like underbrush.

Courageous women started a new conversation surrounding an often silenced or dismissed subject. Not only were they talking about misconduct and abuse; they were talking about *power*.

Sexual assault is not just about oversexed minds inundated with pornographic ideas; it's about power dynamics between men and women in this country (and many others). And you need to look no further than the words of the whistleblowers. The vast majority of the those who spoke out during the #MeToo movement used the word "power" to describe the misconduct and harassment they experienced in the workplace and beyond.[1] These brave women expanded the conversation beyond banal, insufficient words like "misconduct" and helped us understand what was really going on: an abuse of power.

In the aftermath of nearly every accusation, there was an apology. I read nearly all of them. For some reason, public apologies fascinate me. It could be because I'm a pastor, or it could be a more sinister aspect of my character that wants to see someone grovel, but whatever the reason, hearing how people in power apologize (or don't) says a lot about them and a lot about us. Still, during this wave of regrets, there was one apology that received more attention than others.

Louis C.K. was accused by five women of sexual misconduct in November of 2017.[2] His response to the allegations, which came just one day later, garnered more scrutiny than others, perhaps for its length (it's around five hundred words,

1. For a more educated approach to the power dynamics at play in sexual assault and the #MeToo movement, see Yonack, "Sexual Assault Is about Power."

2. Ryzik, Buckley, and Kantor, "Louis C.K. Is Accused by 5 Women of Sexual Misconduct."

nearly a page long, single spaced), but also for its content. He is frank ("These stories are true") and remorseful ("I've brought anguish . . . pain to my family"), but he also does not formally and simply say he is sorry. Because of his omission of the words "I'm sorry" or "I apologize" or anything of that sort, the internet (our new unofficial town mob taken to the global scale) thunderously denounced the apology as not fitting their unwritten standards. The pitchforks were out.

But C.K.'s pseudoapology included a very interesting admission the other apologies I read did not: he was specific. In nearly mirroring the language of his accusers, C.K. pointedly referred to the dynamics of *power* at work in his misconduct: "The power I had over these women is that they admired me," he wrote. "And I wielded that power irresponsibly. I have been remorseful of my actions."[3]

Without wading into the question of whether this is a true apology, we know one thing it is: a clear understanding of his wrongdoing. Whether or not he is sorry about it or feels bad about it, Louis C.K. knows the root of his issue was his relationship with *power*. He had it. The women did not. And he used it not to help them but to harm them.

The great and somewhat unnoticed work of the women who came forward with such courage was their ability to clearly lay out the power dynamics going on, causing every decent man in America—the few remaining—to rethink how they have treated (and continue to treat) women in their life. It was a revelation of the abuses of power in the most sinister ways. After the accusations, many men were thinking publicly about power and their relationship with it for the

3. C.K., "Louis C.K. Responds to Accusations: 'These Stories Are True.'"

first time. "If you would have said to me, 'sexual harassment in the work place is a big deal,' I'd say, 'yeah that's probably true,'" said Ta-Nehisi Coates. "But I didn't know it was like *this*."[4]

The strange thing about power is that you always notice when you *don't* have it, but you rarely notice when you do. This is the entire basis for the "white privilege" discussion. For many years in America, white people have not understood the power they wield. Those in power have a difficult time realizing the power they have, which leads them to use it in manipulative ways that bring harm to those without it. This isn't to excuse or absolve any person in power as if "they had no idea" and so they're not responsible. It's just to show how sneakily our own wickedness surfaces. We *easily* fall into such forms of evil and abuse. We're *that* destructive.

But when you *don't* have power, the power dynamics could not be clearer. You're *certain* you don't have power, and you're fully aware of who has it. When you're rich, you rarely think about how that affects the poor, but when you're poor, you're very aware of how those who are rich exploit you. As a white guy, I do not naturally come to an understanding of my own power in this country until I talk with a person of color. My brothers and sisters of color *absolutely* know the kind of power I have.[5] And just like the women who spoke up and

4. Maron, "Ta-Nehisi Coates."
5. I have heard Tim Keller tell this great story about being a young, white seminary student and discussing race/privilege with a fellow student who was African American. Keller says his friend told him the problem with white people is that we don't think we have a culture. We just think what we do is "normal" and "the way it is." This is precisely the problem at the center of white privilege: assuming what we do is normal and good and the way things go. But when white culture is the dominant culture with the dominant power, we won't have to have it questioned unless we lay it down and elevate the cultural voices around us. The

caused men to think, the other vulnerable groups teach us more about power than any expert in the field.

Here, then, is the relationship between power and vulnerability: the only way to understand the power we hold is by accessing vulnerability. By doing this, we are able to see the places of power we did not previously know existed.

All Around Us

Power is everywhere. The dynamics play out not just in headlines like the #MeToo movement but in our workplaces, homes, families, friendships, and definitely in our churches. The trick is to have the eyes to see. Power dynamics are often disguised.

In churches, for example, it's often people *other than the pastor* who have tons of power. They're influential donors, longtime members, or maybe people with magnetic personalities. Whenever I join a new church, it is always fascinating to me to discover these secretly powerful people. Sometimes these secret power holders are destroying the church and rotting it like some horrendous bacteria, but in other situations they're the life force of the congregation.

I think of Wes, an older member at one of my first churches. Wes and his wife had attended the church for over forty years. They passed out bulletins and served where there was a need, which often had Wes fixing toilets or re-siding the old church building off of Tenth Street. When I met him, Wes wasn't an elder, he wasn't on staff, and he had no official "leadership

---

practical step in this is for us white folks to shut up and listen, to serve more instead of leading so much. To hear Keller's exact comments regarding his personal story, see Keller, "Lecture 2" (the story starts at the 7:15 mark).

position." But Wes was powerful. His humility and willingness to serve gave him a major voice to us who were in leadership. He wielded the power God had given him well, and he led others to do the same, not by coercion, but by love and example.

Power—like money—is not inherently bad. Power can be used for good, and power can be used for evil. But there's one thing we must be clear on: power is everywhere. And people are trying to grab it.

The World's Power

Jeffrey Pfeffer is a professor at Stanford University's prestigious Graduate School of Business. His book *Power: Why Some People Have It—and Others Don't* explores the relationships we have at work and the power at play within them. Pfeffer argues that without power, there will be no success. His tips to his students and readers involve gaining power at any cost. He instructs people to harbor emotions and hold back any vulnerability in meetings if it would cause you to lose power. Remaining confident—even if you're not—is the secret to gaining power, says Pfeffer. And if you want to be successful, you've got to grab power.[6]

"Systematic empirical research confirms what . . . stories, as well as common sense and everyday experience, suggest: being politically savvy and seeking power are related to career success."[7] In America, there is no success without power, and getting this power is all in your control.

6. Pfeffer unpacks a lot of this in his book *Power*; he explains his tactics more succinctly and simply in this short video on the Stanford Graduate School of Business YouTube channel: https://www.youtube.com/watch?v=AozJ4AkgAMw.
7. Pfeffer, *Power*, 4.

It's not difficult to comprehend just how right Pfeffer is about power. We see the awful effects of such logic everywhere: in totalitarian regimes, cults, cutthroat tech companies here in the Silicon Valley, and yes, even (and maybe, especially) in our churches. *This is the way it works*, we think. And we'd better play along with the game if we're going to get ahead. In a world where only the fittest of us will survive, we'd better get to work at taking all the power we can if we want to thrive.

It is not surprising, then, that behind every success story in America, there's a story about power. From Wall Street to Silicon Valley, the so-called leadership experts may not outright tell you they used a certain level of politicking to get to the top, but they did. Pfeffer notes, "Most books by well-known executives . . . touting their own careers as models to be emulated frequently gloss over the power plays they actually used to get to the top."[8] Power is always at work, and our wielding of it will determine our success and happiness.

In America, we want to believe this story, because it is so deeply woven into our cultural narratives. Phrases like "rags to riches" and "pulling yourselves up by your own bootstraps" all come from the stories we love to hear and tell. We want to believe that by sheer willpower we can get what we want. This is often strangely called "the pursuit of happiness."[9]

8. Pfeffer, *Power*, 11.
9. It's strange that a movie by the same name but with a different spelling (starring Will Smith) is about a man changing his socioeconomic status, which, in the story, leads to his "happiness." At least that is how most viewers see the movie superficially. The better reading of this story is how adversity and perseverance irreversibly developed admirable character traits in a man and his son, which ended up bonding the two of them and creating a sustainable and generous life,

Power must be possessed, taken, and assumed if we want to make anything of ourselves—there's no way toward a successful life without being powerful.

Or is there?

Another Way

The journalist Andy Crouch writes about meeting a World Vision leader named Jayakumar Christian in impoverished southeastern India. Jayakumar and his team have very few resources, and as the leader and head of staff, Jayakumar wears ragged clothes. He drives a beat-up car to his various aid sites, and his nonprofit has few supporters and never abounds in finances. And yet, as Crouch follows him around the villages he serves, he makes the observation: "Jayakumar is a powerful man. . . . In a place where power had been abused for generations, Jayakumar and his staff represented a very different kind of power. This power was actually giving life rather than constricting it."[10] Is the only way to power the way of the Stanford Graduate School of Business? Can we only have power if we take control of it, harness it, and grasp after it? Or is there, as Crouch notes, a different kind of power?

This man Crouch met had a unique power. People in his community trusted him, he was reliable, and they would defend him if any accusation came his way. He could influence local issues and help those in need. And yet he wasn't

---

not a greedy one. The film unfortunately casts those in poverty as the victims of bad choices and bad luck, not systemic issues of injustice. The fact that the main character is an African American is also mostly overlooked by white audiences. See Dargis, "Climbing Out of the Gutter with a 5-Year-Old in Tow."

10. Crouch, *Playing God*, 23–24.

in office and received a small salary for a job in the nonprofit sector. What kind of power is this?

Jesus was the most powerful man to ever live. His influence outweighs every celebrity, academic, entertainer, athlete, politician, artist, or leader in all of history. His words have been translated into over a thousand different languages, and billions of people worship him to this day. He is, without a doubt, the most influential and powerful person this world has ever seen.

And Jesus didn't own a company. He never led a staff. His ministry—based out of a small, Roman-occupied city lacking in ethnic and cultural diversity—lasted about three years, during which he traveled less than three hundred miles. He never wrote a book, and he never formally organized his followers. He was, by all accounts, poor, and he worked for most of his life as a stonemason of sorts, sleeping in borrowed rooms. He didn't own any property and never formally organized the movement he started. His life ended when he was convicted in an unjust court system and crucified by an angry mob of religious fundamentalists and their leaders. He died with very few friends to attend to his burial, and his body was laid in a borrowed grave.

And yet no one is more powerful today than Jesus Christ. Billions of people adhere to his words and claim to follow him. Did Jesus take the route outlined by the world's leading experts? Was he "politically savvy," grabbing authority and recognizing power dynamics in order to get ahead?

Considering all of the data we have on his life, we can be sure Jesus did nothing of the sort, and his story is a counternarrative to the one told in the West. A fresh listening to the way Jesus related to power would not just do us great good, it could help save a society addicted to climbing the ladder at all costs.

The Teaching of Jesus: Lords and Servants

Jesus' teaching was marked by his great attention to the poor and forgotten. His most famous sermon—the Sermon on the Mount—begins like this: "Blessed are the poor in spirit" (Matt. 5:3). Jesus gives his "blessing" or benediction to groups like this: the meek, the persecuted, those who mourn, and so on.

Many of us have little understanding of the very churchy word "blessed." In Jesus' language, it is a term of benediction and honor, a way of showing where the favor of God lands. In his time, like ours, those who had a lot of wealth and power were assumed to be "blessed." They were the ones who had access to God.

But the Sermon on the Mount is a grand reordering of the world in light of Jesus' coming (Matt. 5:1–16). Because he has arrived on the scene, Jesus shows us a new way of seeing the world. His order—while it may at first appear upside down when compared to our order—is the true path to life. To Jesus, the rich do not "inherit the earth," the meek do. The powerful are not related to God, but "the peacemakers" are called "sons [and daughters] of God." The happy and sleek and smiling are not the ones "comforted," but those who mourn receive God's sustaining peace.

Again, this seems totally upside down to us. In our ordering of the world, the rich, powerful, healthy, and happy are the ones who are first—they're the ones who get it all. But who is "well-off" in Jesus' world, in his "kingdom"? The poor, persecuted, mourning, and meek. Those are the ones with the "good life."[11] This is how Jesus saw the world. He saw the people we put on the bottom as those at the top. As he famously said, "The last will be first" (Matt. 20:16).

It's no surprise, then, that Jesus quite often interacted with "the scum of the world" (1 Cor. 4:13). He was always eating with tax collectors and "sinners," which were broad categories of people whom the general culture despised (Matt. 9:10–11; Luke 7:34). He gravitated toward those with racial and ethnic backgrounds different than his, and he paid more attention to women than any other religious leader during his time, or sadly, maybe even today. Jesus' focus was on the people at the bottom, not just because he loved them (which he did), but because he understood that they were the ones who would lead the parades in heaven.[12] They secretly held a different kind of power.

11. A lot of this language, including but not limited to the phrases in quotes, is from Dallas Willard's masterpiece, *The Divine Conspiracy*, particularly from chapter 4, entitled "Who Is Really Well Off?—The Beatitudes."

12. This is a reference to the wonderful short story by Flannery O'Connor, "Revelation," from *Everything That Rises Must Converge*. In the story, the grouchy Mrs. Turpin is in a doctor's waiting room. She takes particular note of a "fat girl" about nineteen years old who is reading a book entitled *Human Development* and a "white-trash woman." The fat girl and the woman listen in as Mrs. Turpin rants and raves about the races and classes she considers inferior to herself, spouting off horrific racial slurs and epithets. The girl is disgusted as she complains using phrases at which the reader will continually cringe. When the girl has had enough, she throws the book (the title, *Human Development*, is now ironic) and hits Mrs. Turpin in the head. Mrs. Turpin goes unconscious (or perhaps into a higher state of consciousness?) and receives a vision or "revelation." Near the end of the story, after she has returned home, she sees another, fuller vision:

> She saw the streak as a vast swinging bridge extending upward from the earth through a field of living fire. Upon it a vast horde of souls were tumbling toward heaven. There were whole companies of white trash, clean for the first time in their lives, and bands of black n****rs in white robes, and battalions of freaks and lunatics shouting and clapping and leaping like frogs. And bringing up the end of the procession was a tribe of

Beyond his affinity for vulnerable people groups, Jesus explicitly taught his disciples to follow in a similar manner. In one of his clearest teachings on power and authority, Jesus explains to his disciples how they will not lead their movement the way others have led theirs. The disciples are told not to gain power but to lose it in service to others. In a short scene, two brothers approach Jesus and ask to "sit [at his] right hand and . . . left" (Mark 10:37). This was an ancient Near Eastern way of asking for cabinet positions in Jesus' spiritual government. They wanted the power—and they were doing what the world told them (and tells us) to do: Grab it! It's yours for the taking, so get after it!

Jesus' reply is stunning: "You know that those who are considered rulers of the Gentiles lord it over them, and their great ones exercise authority over them. *But it shall not be so among you*. But whoever would be great among you must be your servant, and whoever would be first among you must be slave of all. For even the Son of Man came not to be served but to serve, and to give his life as a ransom for many" (Mark 10:42–45, emphasis mine).

The "Gentiles" in this passage could be more broadly seen as those who do not follow the one true God. Jesus clearly says, "It shall not be so among you." In other words, you and I will not relate to power the same way the rest of humanity

---

people whom she recognized at once as those who, like herself and Claud, had always had a little of everything and the given wit to use it right. She leaned forward to observe them closer. They were marching behind the others with great dignity, accountable as they had always been for good order and common sense and respectable behavior. They alone were on key. Yet she could see by their shocked and altered faces that even their virtues were being burned away. (217–18)

I read this when I was eighteen years old, and the image has been burned in my brain ever since. A lovely, if haunting, picture of Jesus' order of the universe.

relates to power. In the culture's path to power, it will be to "lord it over" others, to assume power, to grab hold of the reins and take control. But in Jesus' structure of life, his disciples will be the servants and slaves. To continue his theme of an upside-down kingdom, Jesus is telling us: the way up is down. To get to the heights of power, you must "go low."[13] If you want to be great, you serve. The path toward true power and leadership begins in a kind of humiliation.

But what kind of leader tells his disciples to become slaves and servants?

According to the leading experts of today and certainly the leading experts of Jesus' day, the way to success and happiness is through the chain of command. You've got to climb the ladder. Is Jesus setting his disciples up for failure and humiliation? Is this kind of teaching something we should follow in the twenty-first century? How do we know this is true?

The Life of Jesus: Becoming Nothing

We know Jesus' words about leadership are true because of the testimony not only of his teaching but also of his life. The thing about the life of Jesus is that he not only taught wonderful things, but his life was also constantly referring back to his teaching—they never separate. Jesus commands us to do only what he has already done in our place first.

The gospel story of Jesus is this: God became man, dwelt among us, and didn't come lording his power over us, but laid his power down in death so that we might have new life. Of

---

13. The phrase "go low" is taken from John Piper's sermon "For His Sake and Your Joy, Go Low."

all the beings in the universe, God had the right to "lord it over" us—to assume power and control through manipulative acts. He's God, after all. He is the one being with whom we cannot argue. He could have demonstrated his great power by arriving on the scene and destroying us, proving himself as the Mighty One—and he would have been justified in doing so.

But he didn't. And the apostle Paul, an early convert and leader in the Christian church, penned these incredible words about what God did instead: "Jesus . . . , though he was in the form of God, did not count equality with God a thing to be grasped, *but emptied himself, by taking the form of a servant*, being born in the likeness of men. And being found in human form, *he humbled himself* by becoming obedient to the point of death, even death on a cross" (Phil. 2:6–8, emphasis mine).

When God showed up in our world, he not only taught us the secret to true power; he lived it. Instead of arriving in a blaze of heavenly glory, he showed up as a baby born to a poor family in a barn on the outskirts of town. He lived a life of limitations as a human being, constantly laying down his rights as God in order to serve us, the needy and vulnerable ones. True power and authority do not come through job titles, salaries, or circumstances. The most powerful people in our lives are those who have, in vulnerability and humility, laid their life down for us, just like their Creator.

Powerful People in Our Lives

The secret about power is that it is given, not taken. You give power to people all the time. You pick and choose from the gamut of advice your friends give you, and you listen to some people at work more easily than others. Any true spiritual leader in your life has not been assigned to you, but rather they've earned a kind of prominence through their demonstration of humility. The people with the most power in your life—the people you'd follow no matter what—have all *received* such power from you as they've laid their life down on your behalf. In a way, they acted out the gospel for you.

Think about it: someone started listening to you; someone took interest in you; one of your friends has given more time and effort to you than others; one boss at work is easier to take orders from than another because they understand what you do more than the other. All over our lives, we know true power and authority is given to those who have humbly laid their life down for us in some way.

This is the secret Jesus understood. He knew if he came with dominion, there would be rebels. But if he laid his life down for us, there would be converts. He became nothing so we could be something. His death brought us life. If he laid down what he had, we can lay down what we have.

Following Jesus in Humility and Vulnerability

This is the start of the great Christian virtue of humility. By "humility" I mean an accurate self-perception before God.[14] Humility is all about understanding how small and finite

14. I must add here that I agree with Dr. Robert C. Roberts, who wrote, "Accurate self-perception doesn't *guarantee* humility. It's not the same thing as humility, though we sometimes mistake the one for the other." But while accurate self-perception isn't all you need for humility, I would also say that you cannot have humility *without* an accurate self-perception. It is a necessary ingredient in becoming like Jesus. An accurate sense of self *begins* our life of humility and

we are in the grand scheme of things. Humility is not self-deprecation but self-understanding, which—when seen most clearly—leads us to see how little our "self" actually matters.

"Vulnerability" is an expression of humility. To be vulnerable is to share our understanding of our shortcomings with others, ourselves, and God. True vulnerability will always lead us toward connecting with other people because, as Brené Brown writes, "Vulnerability is bankrupt on its own terms when people move from *being* vulnerable to *using* vulnerability to deal with unmet needs, get attention, or engage in the shock-and-awe behaviors that are so commonplace in today's culture."[15] When vulnerability is working best, it's not serving itself, but serving us toward our path of character transformation.

This path toward true power is difficult, but Jesus has gone before us and can show us the way. And so can others. After Jesus' life, there's a multitude of faithful Christians who have experienced the kind of power that comes when we humble ourselves.

For their book *The Way of the Dragon or the Way of the Lamb: Searching for Jesus' Path of Power in a Church That*

---

will constantly fuel it. While self-perception does not "guarantee humility," it certainly sets us up perfectly for it. See Roberts, "Self-Perception and Humility."

15. Brown, *Daring Greatly*, 46. The teaching on vulnerability by Dr. Brown is incredibly helpful, but ultimately not theological. As a theologian and pastor, I just don't think she goes far enough and must agree with Goggin and Strobel, who share their critiques in *The Way of the Dragon and the Way of the Lamb*. Vulnerability has been worshiped as the end goal of much of evangelical community life for the past twenty years or so. We often think that "being vulnerable" with one another is all we have to do when we're in a small-group Bible study. If we cry during a church event and share something honest, we think we've achieved maximum spiritual growth. But, as Brett McCracken points out in "Has 'Authenticity' Trumped Holiness?," vulnerability is not the end goal of Christian life: holiness is. Being like Jesus is more important than "being vulnerable." While vulnerability is an essential step in Christian maturity, becoming Christlike is our aim.

Has Abandoned It, Pastor Jamin Goggin and Dr. Kyle Strobel interviewed influential Christian leaders about power. They talked with J. I. Packer, Dallas Willard, John Perkins, and many others about the nature of their positions as leaders in relationship to the biblical teaching of power. In one section, the two men travel to France to meet with Jean Vanier, the Catholic philosopher and founder of the L'Arche movement, which is a group of thirty-seven communities for the disabled all over the world. Vanier was the mentor of Henri Nouwen, whom I mentioned in the chapter on fame. Vanier was the one who influenced Nouwen to take the path of "downward mobility," a phrase coined by the two.

In the interview with Strobel and Goggin, Vanier summarizes his theory of power this way: "When you admire people, you put them on pedestals. When you love people, you want to be together."[16] In order to be together, Vanier argues, we must come to grips with our weaknesses and difficulties—we must access our humility and vulnerability. "We cannot really begin to know the truth of ourselves until we discover we have difficulties," Vanier says. "Community is the place where we discover our own fragilities, wounds, and inability to love, where our limitations, our fears, and our egoism are revealed to us. We cannot get away from the negative in ourselves. We have to face it. So community life brings a painful revelation of our limitations, weaknesses, and darkness, and the unexpected discovery of the monsters within us."[17]

Christians living in the American Story of More must be fiercely committed to vulnerability and humility within their

16. Goggin and Strobel, *The Way of the Dragon or the Way of the Lamb*, 111.
17. Goggin and Strobel, *The Way of the Dragon or the Way of the Lamb*, 110.

respective local communities. This is the path forward. In workplaces where we're taught to lie to each other and hide our feelings, Christians will live differently. As Americans commit to climbing the corporate ladder, we will serve those at the bottom, knowing that's where we find the abundant life. There's no position of power that will satisfy our broken hearts. Only in sitting at a table in vulnerability will we find true life, because God is not always in the most obvious places of power. If his earthly life told us anything, Jesus would rather be under the overpass than in the Oval Office. He knew something we're trying to ignore: true power is with the poor, the weak, and the vulnerable.

This might explain the Bible's suspicion of empires. For the past number of years, I've had the privilege of lecturing on the book of Daniel to college students on the Oregon coast. Daniel is a book all about national power. And yet, chapter after chapter (and vision after vision—Daniel is *full* of visions), the book gives the same message: kings and kingdoms will come and go; God's heavenly kingdom will be the only one to last. The Babylonians are scary, but they'll soon be artifacts. The Greeks may appear powerful, but their impressive structures will be ruins in no time. Over and over, it's the same story throughout all of history: the powerful are only powerful for a time. Someday, the ruins of the White House will be a tourist attraction.

We, "the most powerful country on earth," can learn humility from the Bible's treatment of power. America has the largest military in the history of the world, we have a dominant economy, but *are we really that powerful?* In one sense we are; in another sense we're incredibly fragile, one cyberattack away from losing it all. I've often found myself in a third-world country, where no one has a Social Security number or a bank account password, thinking, *everyone here is so free.*

While we stress about who is president and "what is happening to this country," we may be forgetting where the action is in God's mind. All over the world, the meek and humble are serving. Our attention may be on the American kingdom, but could it be that the more impoverished of our brothers and sisters are "first" in God's kingdom? One day, God will show our pecking order to be upside down. As Christians, our choice is with whom we will stand. To place ourselves with the poor and humble gives us the opportunity to be like them, to be like Jesus.

This kind of living will lead us to abundant life because it's the kind of life Jesus lived. We will be happier as we practice vulnerability. We will find joy in the slums instead of the conference rooms atop cityscapes. From what I've seen, there's more life, freedom, and hope in the ghetto than in the Silicon Valley. A kind of power exists with those who, at first glance, have none but, on deeper inspection, have more than you could possibly imagine. It's just harder to see when our bank account is steady. And that means we need to talk about where the American Story of More finally leads us: to a pile of cash.

Wealth and Generosity

Here we don't die, we shop.

DON DELILLO, *White Noise*

Think, for a second, about explaining escalators.

Imagine yourself in the position of someone like Sasha, who leads orientation classes for Sudanese refugees in Atlanta. To start, due to a massive change in climate, you have to explain snow by passing around an ice cube to the amazement of these young men and women from a country that rarely experiences temperatures under sixty degrees Fahrenheit. But you also have to tell them about escalators.

And how would you answer this very simple question from the orientation class: "Why do you need the stairs to move? Can't you just walk?"

This question would come, perhaps, from a young man who walked over two hundred miles through the jungle at the age of seven in order to escape his country's violence. How would you answer that question?[1] I guess our only answer is an embarrassing one: we . . . don't want to walk?

Whoever invented the escalator, there is no doubt it was made in a culture of remarkable wealth, like something a king would order to be conceived,[2] tired of walking and maybe unable to because of gross weight gain. The escalator—like many Western inventions—was made not out of necessity, but opulence.

Now take this same line of thinking across numerous inventions and developments in technology—how much of what we have right now was made *out of necessity*? When you travel to the third world, become friends with the poor, or simply listen to your neighbors who have less than you do and always will, you cannot help but see how much of what we have is truly unnecessary. Think about what you would need for survival out of your home or apartment, and it is

1. This example of Sasha's orientation class is not hypothetical, but is mentioned in a short section on p. 18 of Dave Eggers's book *What Is the What?* The book is a novel but is based almost entirely on the true story of Valentino Achak Deng, one of thousands of "Lost Boys of Sudan." Deng, like other Lost Boys, walked for hundreds of miles to escape the country's violence. This book, along with others, faithfully tells one of the great survival stories at length, but also unpacks the difficulties of surviving in America as a refugee. For Deng and many others, escaping violence and oppression in their home country is just the first phase of survival, with the second being the survival of life in America as a refugee. *What Is the What?* helped me consider how the second phase of survival might be just as difficult as the first.

2. The escalator was, in fact, born amidst tremendous privilege right after the Industrial Revolution in America. The history appears to be a bit fuzzy, but the patent and early models come from rich, educated white men living in the Northeastern United States (Nathan Ames, Leamon Souder, Jesse Reno, George Wheeler, and Charles Seeberger). The Wikipedia entry is actually quite fascinating: https://en.wikipedia.org/wiki/Escalator#Inventors_and_manufacturers.

very little. Moreover, if you were to be placed in a position of survival, most of your devices could only support you until the battery died.

It could be—and perhaps *should be*—argued that for all of our advancement of unnecessary things, we truly have no experience of necessary things. As a character in the Don DeLillo novel *White Noise* puts it:

> It's like we've been flung back in time. . . . Here we are . . . knowing all these great things after centuries of progress but what can we do to make life easier? . . . Can we make a refrigerator? Can we even explain how it works? What is electricity? What is light? We experience these things every day of our lives but what good does it do if we find ourselves hurled back in time and we can't even tell people the basic principles much less actually make something that would improve conditions. Name one thing you could make.[3]

We are fools to convince ourselves that wealth has made us a better species. Could it be that in our technological and financial progress, we have lost basic elements of our humanity? If this is true physically and mentally—if our ability to open a refrigerator has replaced our ability to explain it—how much more true is this spiritually? Wealth *does something to us*—it inoculates us and changes how we think about the world and live inside of it. We no longer consider the absurdity of the escalator. While our wealth has given us remarkable power in this world, are we vulnerable in ways we cannot yet imagine? Has wealth given Americans and those in the wealthy West an Achilles' heel?

3. DeLillo, *White Noise*, 147.

America the Rich?

America is, without a doubt, the richest nation in the history of the world. There has never been more money and more possessions in one place at one time. Even when we balance it with inflation, we've never had a higher GDP, and individuals and families have never made more money.[4]

And this is the goal of the whole American narrative. We start with growth and an addiction to success, but the end goal of our lives—according to the American Dream—is to amass wealth. We want wealth, in fact, so we can stop working for the last years of our lives. We call this "retirement." The American Story is pitched to us, but we rarely think through the ending. Go to school to get good grades, get good grades so you can get a good job, get a good job so you can make money, make money so you can retire, retire so you can golf. Here at the end of your life are acres of lawn where you can learn to hit a ball until you die. But you've got to make enough money first. To be sure, there is much to gain through wealth, even a modest amount of it, but there's also something we lose when we become rich.

The true expense of our wealth (pun intended) has come emotionally and spiritually. A study done by the Pew Research Center revealed that while Americans make far more than any other advanced nation by an average of ten thousand dollars a year, only 41 percent describe their average day as "particularly good," while countries with far less earning potential like Nigeria and Nicaragua report upward of 60 percent claiming most of their days are "good."[5] Money does not buy happiness, even at the daily level.

4. See Sherman, "America Is the Richest, and Most Unequal, Country."
5. Gao, "How Do Americans Stand Out from the Rest of the World?"

This could be because while we have a lot of money, we also *owe* a lot of money. Behind our homes, cars, clothes, and iPhones, there is an ugly amount of debt. As of 2018, the average American with credit card debt has a balance of $15,482—that's the *average*. As for home mortgages, Americans who have a mortgage owe an average of $181,176.[6] And the average student loan debt for the class of 2017 was over $39,000.[7] This means if you're the *average* homeowner with a credit card who went to college in America, you owe various banks over $200,000.[8] Do we really possess the amount of money we say we do? It's all numbers on a screen at some point, floating around and transferring from account number to account number, never really "ours" but always feeling like it. The dollar is a great American farce.

But you wouldn't know this by a quick glance at consumer spending. We love our dollars, even if they're a joke. Every day, the average American consumer spends $100 to $110 on nonessential items.[9] That's just every normal day that we also describe as "not particularly good," according to the research quoted above. For Christmas, Americans spend over $450 billion *every year*. You don't even want to know

6. El Issa, "NerdWallet's 2017 American Household Credit Card Debt Survey."
7. Student Loan Hero, "Shocking Student Loan Debt."
8. A good summary of the above-cited statistics on debt can be found in Martin, *The New Better Off*, which explores the premises of American contentment around money, time, work, and family. Her thesis is an interesting one: Americans are changing in their understanding of what makes a "good life," and this current generation of parents is the first to believe that their children will not be "better off" than them. While Martin gives a compelling vision for what she calls "The New Better Off," as a pastor and theologian, I find her scope limited. Christian thinking always goes beyond the immediate self, its vicinity and local relationships, and even the earth. While Christian thinking is nothing less than that, my work here takes on some larger considerations involving our own historical faith commitments, biblical theology, a person's soul, and the place all of these things have in American life.
9. Statista, "Average Daily Consumer Spending."

how much we spend on Halloween candy.[10] If we spend this much all year only to end the year in massive debt, are we actually "rich"?

And maybe this is the point in the chapter where you're thinking, "OK, but I actually am *not* rich." You could be what we recklessly refer to as a "poor college student." Or you could be working a dead-end job and living paycheck to paycheck. You could be on government assistance. You could be struggling every day. And still—and I say this with hesitation, knowing the various circumstances many of you may be in—you are, by the world's standard, "rich" if you can flush a toilet. To have running water puts you in the richest 5 percent of the world.[11] We have to think this globally and this creatively to understand just how deep our obsession with wealth goes.

The American mentality of spending ourselves into debt reveals something essential to our national character: We *love* money. We *worship* money. If you think that is too dramatic of language, just think about what those words mean. At the heart of love and worship is service and honor. When viewed through this lens, is it possible we love *and* serve money?

Money, Religion, and the Soul

When a pastor starts talking about money, you can feel the congregation cringe. For the past ten years as a pastor in America, I can tell you I have *always* received criticism

10. OK, you do: we spent $9.1 billion on Halloween costumes and candy in 2017. See Leasca, "Here's the Very Scary Amount of Money Americans Spend on Halloween."

11. Alcorn, *Money, Possessions, and Eternity*, 291.

whenever talking about money. No matter the age demographic or the socioeconomic background, when you mention money in a sermon, the room goes strangely silent.

Likewise, when counseling people, money is a touchy subject because we generally believe none of our life is interconnected and our money problems have nothing to do with our faith problems. We believe buying a car has nothing to do with what we have deemed our "spiritual life." By exiling our spiritual life to its own private island, we can safely do whatever we want with our money and maintain what we refer to as a "relationship with God." And that's why we get uncomfortable when the pastor talks about money. We're certain he'll somehow infringe on our neatly compartmentalized life and command us to give to his church.

I don't blame people for this criticism. The church must own its past and present sins regarding money. Too many stories of pastors becoming incredibly wealthy through the widow's mite have led those of us in America to a place of deep skepticism. It's just a consequence of former sins.

And still, it's strange, isn't it? Money is a touchy subject. You don't talk about it with people you barely know, and you shouldn't bring it up at the dinner table. What we do with our money is a private affair ("my business," we say) that no one else needs to be involved in because, in America, we view it as "our money."

But let me ask: Could our discomfort with the topic of money reveal our deep love of it? Is it possible that we are so uncomfortable with the Bible's teaching on money because we love it so much? It's funny: when I preach on the topic of money in the Bible, I am never criticized by generous people.

Scripture's Skepticism of Money

Jesus talked more about money than any other topic save "the kingdom of God." He talked more about money than forgiveness or grace or love or justice. If we took only Jesus' words about money, we could do what others have done: write a whole book on just that. But instead, we should use this fact of Jesus' mass of teaching on money to launch into some appropriate questions.

Why would Jesus talk so much about money? If Jesus was a spiritual teacher or God himself or an important human being, wouldn't it be foolish to ignore his statements? If he was who he said he was—God—could our Creator be telling us something essential about life by repeating so much on one subject? Finally, where else in the Bible could Jesus' statements about money lead us? Perhaps the Christian message has something to say about Americans' great love of money.

This is where we must make a distinction between money and the love of money. When taking the totality of Scripture's teaching on money, we can see that it does not reject money and teach asceticism, but it also doesn't fully embrace money and teach hedonism.[12] The apostle Paul famously warns Timothy, "For the *love of money* is a root of all kinds of evils. It is through this craving that some have wandered away from the faith and pierced themselves with many pangs" (1 Tim. 6:10, emphasis mine). Jesus himself

---

12. I can hear my John Piper fans standing up in defiance now. I'll just say this: I agree with Piper that "God is most glorified when we are most satisfied in Him," but I reject his use of the word "hedonism," which has a much richer history around opulence and self-gratification, leaving it unhelpful in our teaching and preaching to twenty-first-century Americans. To me, the word's etymology is not something to be redeemed or used in the church.

simply states, "Beware! Guard against *every kind of greed*. Life is not measured by how much you own" (Luke 12:15 NLT, emphasis mine). The deepest warnings of Scripture regarding money are not that *money* is evil, but that we are. Money just reveals that. The mass accumulation of money simply puts us at a spiritual disadvantage because we are much more likely to fall into greed. Greed deals not with how much money we have, but with our relationship to it. This is the Bible's primary concern: our devotion.

A Battle of Devotions

This is why the best summary of the Bible's invitation to us regarding money is found in the ancient book of Proverbs. This Hebrew collection of wisdom served as a booklet for parents to take their children through as they came through puberty. It's full of great advice on the main subjects young people struggle with: sex, work, God, and money. And it's in this book that this prayer arrives:

> Two things I ask of you;
>> deny them not to me before I die:
> Remove far from me falsehood and lying;
>> give me neither poverty nor riches;
>> feed me with the food that is needful for me,
> lest I be full and deny you
>> and say, "Who is the LORD?"
>> or lest I be poor and steal
>> and profane the name of my God. (Prov. 30:7–9)

Summarizing the Bible's message for wealth, this Wisdom writer asks God to give him "neither poverty nor riches."

Somewhere in between the massive love for money and the pride of asceticism is the Bible's teaching on a decent wage responsibly earned. But before we start thinking we're in the clear spiritually if we're "middle class" (a class nearly 70 percent of Americans consider themselves to be),[13] let's look a bit closer to see *why* this writer would ask God for not too little and not too much.[14]

At the end of this proverb, the writer says he desires to be protected from the dangers of wealth not only so he won't forget God ("lest I be full and deny you") in worship of possessions, but also so he won't use God's name in vain ("profane the name of my God") if he were poor. The root of the prayer is the author's *devotion*: will it be to God or to something else? The philosopher Dallas Willard summarizes it this way: "The most important commandment of the Judeo-Christian tradition is to treasure God and his realm more than anything else. That is what it means to love God. . . . It means to treasure him."[15] Of primary concern for the proverb writer is his relationship with his Creator, and he wisely understands how wealth can compromise it, leaving the soul empty and wanting for more instead of being satisfied with God. We see once again that the issue is not with money but with our relationship to it.

"The problem, of course, is not that God doesn't love the rich," writes Randy Alcorn. "The problem is that the rich

13. Martin, "Nearly 70% of Americans."

14. The New Testament scholar Craig L. Blomberg uses this proverb to title his book *Neither Poverty nor Riches* (which is one of the best biblical theologies of money and possessions). For those more interested in a strict theology of possessions and money, I highly recommend this book, although it is quite academic. More popular readers would be best suited with Randy Alcorn's *Money, Possessions, and Eternity*. And one certainly could not lose by reading both.

15. Willard, *The Divine Conspiracy*, 203.

don't love God. They simply have too much else to love. Who needs God, we think, when we've got everything."[16] Jesus' primary teachings on money have to do with devotion and service (Matt. 6:24; 19:23–24). In Matthew 6:24, when Jesus plainly says human beings cannot serve two masters, that "you cannot serve God and money," the word he uses for "money" is the Greek term *mammon*, which is better translated as "stuff" or "possessions."[17] Serving God is nearly impossible the more you accumulate stuff. The Bible is full of examples of unchecked prosperity breeding thankless-ness and pride within the human heart (Deut. 6:1–15; 31:20; 2 Chron. 26:6–16; Ps. 49:5–6; Hosea 13:4–6; 1 Tim. 6:10). But apart from our "class" standing, how will we know if we serve *mammon* or not?

The Litmus Test

Certainly it's easy to arrange our lives with specific religious disciplines in order to appear devoted to God, all the while amassing wealth and falling in love with our stuff. Thank-fully, Jesus provides one of the simplest litmus tests for those of us seeking to understand our greed: "Where your treasure is, there your heart will be also" (Matt. 6:21).

16. Alcorn, *Money, Possessions, and Eternity*, 42. Almost all of this section needs to include a huge tip of the hat to Randy Alcorn, one of the best writers on and examples of the Bible's teaching on money. Not only did he write one of the best theologies of possessions (in the book quoted here and throughout this chapter: *Money, Possessions, and Eternity*), but he and his wife have lived a tremendous example. Alcorn gives 100 percent of his proceeds from his books to charitable organizations. He makes minimum wage and lives simply, while his books, collectively, have sold millions of copies. He's also an Oregonian, which makes me proud.

17. See Blomberg, *Neither Poverty nor Riches*, 132.

Locate your treasure and you'll find your heart's desire. But what is our treasure? We could equate this term "treasure" with our time and our money, our calendars and our bank accounts. These are very good items to put in this test, because they never lie. If you look back on your last week and see how you spent every minute of every day, you would learn something. Likewise, most adults have experienced the frustration of reviewing their bank statements. By examining our calendars and our spending habits, we see clearly what we treasure most. We cannot lie in the face of such obvious math: locate your treasure, and you'll find your heart.

Has America chosen its devotion? Where is the heart of America? Looking at our habits with our money, it would seem impossible to label us a "Christian nation," as many pompously have. We are not a nation of "Christian values"; we're a nation of consumeristic values.[18]

18. After the horrific events of September 11, 2001, President George W. Bush gave various addresses regarding the state of America after the attacks. Many Americans were paralyzed with fear. People stopped flying for a while, families stockpiled supplies, and New York and other big cities were covered with a blanket of unease. During one of his addresses, just two weeks after the attacks and with the nation still reeling with anxiety, President Bush stood at O'Hare International Airport outside of Chicago and assuaged fears by encouraging Americans to keep shopping. The worry from Washington was that with so many still in fear, consumer spending would drop during the key, forecasted boost between Thanksgiving and Christmas. American life is reliant on consumer spending, and without it, our economic and governmental structures have difficulty operating. For those in Western capitalistic societies, we spend to survive. In his address, President Bush said, "Do your business around the country. Fly and enjoy America's great destination spots. Get down to Disney World in Florida. Take your families and enjoy life, the way we want it to be enjoyed. And we've got a role, the government's got a role. Not only do you have a role to play, which you're playing in such fine fashion, but the government has a role to play, as well. We've got a significant responsibility to deal with this emergency in a strong and bold way. And we are doing so." The role of the United States citizen is clear: spend. The president's remarks have been archived in Bush, "At O'Hare, President Says 'Get On Board.'"

Curing Our Greed

The biblical counter-narrative to such a consumeristic, greedy society is for believers to cultivate a grateful and generous life. Thanksgiving—the practice of speaking your gratitude to God and others—is a rare discipline we *maybe* practice awkwardly once a year around a table of family members with whom we're rarely honest. But the call of the Scriptures is more subversive, more difficult, and more common than a yearly homage. The upside-down way of life is found in the biblical terms of "thanksgiving" and "generosity."

The American Christian must be different from the American non-Christian in that they are to be abounding in thanksgiving for all they have—however little, however much. We should sing along with the psalmist, "The LORD is my shepherd; there is nothing I lack" (Ps. 23:1 HCSB). This contentment leads to deep thankfulness in our hearts for life and everything in it. The Christian should be "abounding in thanksgiving" (Col. 2:7).

Thanksgiving requires imagination. Instead of imagining what we do not have and want, we imagine what life would be like *without what we currently have.* To quote the immortal prophet Sheryl Crow from her hit song "Soak Up the Sun": "It's not having what you want / It's wanting what you've got."[19] Outside of the absurdity of a pop song, the truth cuts through, I hope. A shift in our imagination is required in order

19. Sheryl Crow, "Soak Up the Sun," *C'mon C'mon* (A&M, 2002). I can't believe I'm quoting Sheryl Crow, and I know what I've done to you as the reader: You will be singing this song for most of the next week, annoying the members of your family and perhaps testing some of your closest friendships. But I had to quote it because my father, when he was in his forties and I in my teenage years, would quote this incessantly to us kids. He did this to try to help us understand thankfulness, and in some strange way, I think it worked. So, really, this is on you, Dad.

to be thankful, to see life through the lens of what is currently in our possession and how life would be if it were not.

An easy way to enlarge your imagination in this way is to be friends with those who have difficulty affording American life. It is a goal in our family to make sure we always are in relationship with at least a couple of people who struggle to afford groceries. Jesus taught his followers to remain in close proximity to the poor. They're "blessed." They know something about the value of life and God that the rich do not. The rich know very little about God and face a spiritual disadvantage the more they accumulate. Due to my upbringing, social class, and current socioeconomic status, I certainly identify with the latter, which is why a relationship with the former is so important. The more money you make, the less in touch with God you tend to become. Furthermore, friendship with the poor changes how my wife and I make financial decisions. Sure, we *could* afford this or that, but why would we when our friends need help meeting their most basic needs?

The church remains the great gift in all of this because a good congregation should put you in touch with the less fortunate. Only in the church can the rich and poor come together around communion and both confess, "I am weak and sinful, but only say the word and I shall be healed" (cf. Matt. 8:8). The body of Christ is where we should rub shoulders and share meals with people very different from us in all kinds of ways. This is how we see ourselves clearer, for sure, and also how we see God.

The Catholic priest Ronald Rolheiser writes, "God cannot be related to without continually digesting the uneasiness and pain that are experienced by looking, squarely and honestly, at how the weakest members in our society are faring and how our own lifestyle is contributing to that."[20] There is simply no way to know God fully unless we know the poor. I believe American life would dramatically change if everyone had at least one close relationship with a person experiencing material poverty. While our stock market might be affected and our businesses would not be as profitable, our souls would be lighter and our brothers and sisters in poverty might be lifted out.

From Thanksgiving to Giving

Once you practice thanksgiving, you're quite literally halfway to just "giving." Grateful people give their money and possessions away; they share what they have because they understand it's not theirs. All of life is God's and certainly all of our money is his. What would happen if Americans became more consistently thankful? They'd become consistently generous.

Right now, the average American gives around 3 percent of his or her earnings each year.[21] According to the National Philanthropic Trust, American "individuals, estates, foundations and corporations" gave just over $390 billion in 2017.[22] You may think, "Hey that's pretty good!" but when you compare it to the $450 billion we spent on *just* Christmas, you'll see the issue. Americans are not charitable people, and our country is not generous. If we were to bring that figure of 3 percent up to even 10 percent, the results would be dramatic.

But shaming people into giving is ineffective. Christians have a deep resource to help us understand generosity: the

20. Rolheiser, *The Holy Longing*, 66.
21. See Campbell, "Why Are Americans Less Charitable Than They Used to Be?"
22. See Giving USA, "Giving USA 2017: Total Charitable Donations Rise to New High of $390.05 Billion."

gospel. Jesus Christ "became poor" so that we might "become rich" (2 Cor. 8:9). In the gospel, the spiritually wealthiest Being did not consider such a status "a thing to be grasped . . . but emptied himself" (Phil. 2:6–11). In Jesus, we see the great example of generosity: he gave his whole life. As we stare in gratitude at this, a giving heart emerges.

After such a conversion in the gospel, Christians also understand God to be their greatest treasure. We are wealthy even if we have no material possessions. This is why we can join the host of biblical examples and "freely give" (Deut. 15:10; Ps. 112:9; Prov. 11:24; Matt. 10:8; 1 Cor. 9:18).

Because we are rich in Christ, we do not need to be rich in money. There is no need for self-righteous asceticism, but there is a need for a serious reevaluation of our material possessions. We do not need most of what we have, and we should not get most of what we want. Instead, we should receive what we need with thanksgiving, and give what we do not generously. It is this simple, consistent biblical message that flies in the face of the American Story of More.

If we make more money, our "standard of *giving* should increase, not [our] standard of living."[23] Could Christians lead a reformation of wealth in America, redistributing the money we've received to those who have very little? I think we can.

The Myth of Generosity

The added bonus to moving toward a life of generosity is found in a simple teaching from Jesus: "It is more blessed to give than receive" (Acts 20:35). In this passage, Jesus uses the

23. White, "Four Lessons on Money," quoted in Alcorn, *Money, Possessions, and Eternity*, 299.

Greek word *makarios*, which is most commonly translated "blessed."[24] But alternatively (and maybe more accurately), the word can be translated "happy" or "happy-making." Taking this into consideration, we can see Jesus' teaching now become "It is more happy-making to give than to receive." Beyond this one verse, I believe the Bible equates a generous life with a happy life.

Could part of our depression be not only from our isolation, busyness, and loneliness but also from our selfish uses of our money? Remember, greed is not about how much you have but about your relationship with what you have. If you hold things loosely, then, you'll most likely live a more joyful life. If you hold your things closely, you'll become insufferable. Haven't you seen this on your television?

This might be why you'll never meet an "ex-giver." You'll never come into contact with someone who could be described as "formerly generous." You see, giving is life-giving. When we begin to hold our money and possessions lightly, we become "blessed" or "happy." This is a kind of holy addiction, where the more we give, the more joy we receive. There will never be any feeling like it.

When I wrote my first book, I received a good amount of money for it up front. I've always wanted to be like Francis Chan and Randy Alcorn—both of whom give away 100 percent of their royalties to ministry and charity work all over the country. As I was lining up the contract I thought, *I can't*

24. The best summary of this word is found in Randy Alcorn's terrific book *Happiness*. I was able to take a class from Alcorn at Western Seminary on this subject and this Greek word. His book is an argument for keeping the word "happy" as a part of a Christian's language. It defies the colloquial phrase "God's not interested in your happiness; he's interested in your holiness." Alcorn simply asks, "Couldn't he be interested in both?"

wait to do that one day. I was thinking I would one day sell as many books as them and give hundreds of thousands—or, in their cases, millions—of dollars away. I was getting a couple of thousand for my first book. *One day*, I thought.

But then it hit me—or, should I say, God hit me: "What's the difference?" There's no time like right now to start such a project. I gave my first check for that book away, and the second I saved for our family. In a strange, biblical way, I learned something. The saving felt *good*—I knew it was a wise decision since my wife and I were about to move and I was going to be looking for work—but the giving felt *great*. Now, as I write this book, I pray it serves many more people so I can give all the more, not because I "should" but because I want to—I want that same joy again. I suppose I just can't see myself giving any *less*. And that's exactly it: the joy comes alongside the giving.

Do not think for a second this is easy for anyone, especially me. In my own small way, I hope to live in this kind of counter-narrative. But it is difficult in the Silicon Valley. They say "Money will never buy you happiness," but I often believe a Tesla would. Where we live, wealth is how you survive. It's nearly impossible to live in the Bay Area without having a certain level of wealth. Many of our friends own expensive cars, wear nice clothes, and get a raise with every new job they take. Some days I want that life. But on my better days, when I listen to Jesus, and even when I listen to the data I've presented in this chapter, I *know* great material wealth has a great cost. While being generous and grateful costs us something, I'm afraid greed costs more.

PART 3

The
Implications

Death and Life

I love this town. I think sometimes of going into the ground
here as a last wild gesture of love.

MARILYNNE ROBINSON, *Gilead*

Five miles from my house, in the heart of the Silicon
Valley and just steps away from the Stanford University campus, there are train tracks separating the
center of the city and its major road. In order to get into
downtown Palo Alto, one has to cross these tracks.

When my wife and I first moved to this area, I noticed
something peculiar. Right beside the rail, on the west side
of the tracks, there was a small overhang next to a parked
car where a man sat in a lawn chair. He wore a reflective vest
and held a thermos. He wasn't doing much of anything, just
sitting by the tracks with terrible posture, watching cars go
by. At first I thought he might be homeless, but it was not

an ideal place to beg, with traffic mostly passing by or only momentarily stopping for the commuter train to pass. Plus, his reflective vest made him seem like he had some kind of official status. I drove by many times at different hours, and he would be replaced by all different kinds of people, all doing the same thing—or the same "nothing": sitting in a lawn chair and watching the tracks. There is no station or anyone else close; there is just a person sitting in a lawn chair.

Then my wife came home one day from her clinic rotation and solved the mystery for me. During this time, once a month, my wife worked in an outpatient clinic in Menlo Park, the city next door to Palo Alto. She served families as their primary pediatrician, learning a lot about the diversity in a seemingly homogenously wealthy community.

"Have you seen people sitting by the train tracks in Palo Alto?" she asked.

I nodded. "Yeah. Do you know what they're doing?"

"Those are parents."

She went on to tell me about a major issue in Silicon Valley, one that has been reported on widely by national and international news outlets. Each year, and especially in 2008–2010, around the time of final exams at local high schools in the valley, there is a dramatic increase in teen suicide. And, in one particular year, a sad, dark commonality was found in all of the suicides: the train. This led a group of parents to recruit from among themselves volunteers to watch over the tracks in order to prevent their own children from jumping in front of the oncoming high-speed trains.

When reporter Hanna Rosin investigated teen suicide in Palo Alto for *The Atlantic*, she called her piece "The Silicon Valley Suicides" and wrote, "I've read all these books, and so have many of my friends. We have kids this age, or about to be this age, and yet somehow we can't absorb the message. I didn't, really, until I spent some time in Palo Alto."[1] Under the immense pressure of their community and the overarching story American life was telling them, these kids found it better to jump in front of a train than fail.

The Silicon Valley is the American Dream on steroids. We live and work in an area where people are making more money than ever in the most successful career paths you can imagine. Every day, billions of dollars roll through this little stretch of land and make their way all over the world. Stanford University, which sits in the heart of the valley, remains one of the coveted institutions for applying undergrads, all the more if you go to Palo Alto High School, which sits directly across the street from the university.

Rosin quotes a study finding that "one of the two major causes of distress . . . was the 'pressure to excel at multiple academic and extracurricular pursuits.'"[2] When the students were asked to rank their top ten values, half of all the values cited by every teenager studied had to do with achievement ("attend a good college," "make a lot of money," "excel academically"). The teenagers raised in this environment are put into a kind of pressure cooker by the American Story of More. And if they begin failing at it, they fall into a deep depression, many of them choosing to attempt to take their own life.[3]

1. This deep-dive investigation into local high schools near Palo Alto is devastating and revealing. Rosin explores the racial tension among Asian families as well as the influence the tech industry has had on teenage life.

2. Rosin, "The Silicon Valley Suicides."

3. See Lee, "The Unsettling Truth about What's Hurting Today's Students." In the article, Lee, who is on the faculty at Northeastern University, writes, "In a

The story they're told by parents, coaches, teachers, mentors, family friends, and even their own peers is the one I have told throughout this book. It is a story about endless and ferocious growth at all costs—even life itself. The story is about isolating yourself, "making a name for yourself," and accumulating as much money as possible in order for people to find you respectable. It's a story about growing your company *and* your church *and* your platform, all while your bank account grows. In this story, you can't make less money than your parents and be considered a "success." If your dad went to Stanford, you can't go to junior college. If you're raised in the Silicon Valley, you can't grow up to be poor. You would be what Americans have no category for but pity: a failure. A recent nationwide study on teenagers in wealthy areas "constructed a profile of elite American adolescents whose self-worth is tied to their achievements and who see themselves as catastrophically flawed if they don't meet the highest standards of success."[4]

This is what drives young people into depression all over America, and especially here in the Silicon Valley. And it is, in my estimation, what is killing us. Our country, like the Silicon Valley, has the appearance of life, but a dying and depressed heart. Behind our enormous shopping malls, titans of industry, and success stories, there is another story of deep darkness, one I have done my best to outline here. And make no mistake: this is not a problem of making a better culture or making a better society (although that may happen if we

hyper-competitive market, it would seem sacrilegious to expect our students not to compete with each other, even though research affirms that obsessive ladder climbing can lead to disastrous falls."

4. The study, reported in Rosin, "The Silicon Valley Suicides," was done by Yale's psychiatry department under Suniya Luthar.

correct this story of mass accumulation). No, more is at stake here. I do not think it to be overly dramatic to say that the American Story of More is killing our children—literally. This is an issue of life and death.

Too Dramatic?

Is a sentence like that overly dramatic? Am I sounding the alarm bells after a small cooking mishap, causing the building to evacuate over a little smoke? Perhaps. But even one child throwing themselves in front of a train because they couldn't achieve what their community was asking of them should cause us to think. More so, a statistical pattern in the next generation should promote a national conversation about who we are becoming. For the last ten years, teen suicide in America has been steadily increasing, making it one of the leading causes of death in those between the ages of fifteen and thirty.[5]

But there's something bigger here. "Silicon Valley" has become the same thing as Hollywood or Wall Street: while it began in one place, one location tied to one economy, it has become a global idea, transcending its geography. We talk about "Silicon Valley" in the same way we talk about "Hollywood": a cultural pattern, a way of life, a value system that can manifest anywhere. You do not need to come near where I live to see "the Silicon Valley." In fact, the Silicon Valley is working to make this possible: they want offices everywhere, their employees to be "mobile," and their workspaces to be "virtual." And it's more than the actual companies, it's the culture they're selling of being constantly connected, constantly making money, and growing endlessly.

5. American Foundation for Suicide Prevention, "Suicide Statistics."

There can never be "enough" Facebook users. If Hollywood transported the identity of fame across the world and outside of Los Angeles, and Wall Street galvanized a "greed is good" culture beyond New York City, then Silicon Valley is pushing the American story of mass accumulation and achievement at any cost beyond Palo Alto.

If the drive to achieve, be successful, grow, and gain wealth is affecting this small geographic area right now, how will it affect the other places the "idea" of Silicon Valley travels? We have exported the American Dream through the channel of Silicon Valley values, and if we do not think creatively as Christians, we will continue to sell our souls in order to gain the world. What must we do?

Disruption

The tech industry has a term they love: "disruption." Essentially, disruption happens when a new company creates a new market and value network, disrupting the existing structures in place.[6] This is a company coming out of nowhere to totally change the game of how people make decisions and where money and profits go. In other words, disruption happens when there's one dominant story of how business should be done—one story that all of the books and conferences reinforce—and a new business or product comes along that

6. Here I'll let the Silicon Valley speak for itself. The tech news site *Tech-Crunch*, in an article by Andy Rachleff pompously titled "What 'Disrupt' Really Means," says, "An incumbent in the market finds it almost impossible to respond to a disruptive product. In a new-market disruption, the unserved customers are unserved precisely because serving them would be unprofitable given the incumbent's business model. In a low-end disruption, the customers lost typically are unprofitable for the incumbents, so the big companies are happy to lose them."

says, "No, things are different now." This was what Napster was to the music industry, or Wikipedia to the academic world. These companies radically redefined their industry and its practices.

There is a pattern of life here in America marked by the subjects of this book: greed, endless growth, isolation, fame, and an unhealthy addiction to success. And I am not interested in halting this story. I am not a culture warrior. What I am interested in is Christians *disrupting* it. Christians, by living according to the biblical counter-narrative, can disrupt the American culture machine by asking fundamental questions like "Why do we need our company to get bigger?" and "Does our church need a larger budget?" and "Why do I need more money than what I have right now?" Because the biblical pattern of life is so different from the American pattern, the hope is not to halt or destroy the American Story but to disrupt it—to introduce a new way of life by faithfully living as an example of it.

But this would mean something quite significant. This would mean Christians must die to the American Story. Faithful Christians must now die to the idea that their company, church, or business idea will endlessly grow toward massive wealth, and they must instead begin to focus on faithful observance of pace, obscurity, community, vulnerability, and generosity. In our dying to the American Story, we can begin to live the biblical one.

Death

We saw through the "Silicon Valley Suicides" that there's a kind of life that brings you toward death. The Bible would suggest the opposite is true as well: there's a kind of dying that brings life.

Jesus, in one of his most famous teachings, said, "If anyone would come after me, let him deny himself and take up his cross and follow me. For whoever would save his life will lose it, but whoever loses his life for my sake will find it. For what will it profit a man if he gains the whole world and forfeits his soul? Or what shall a man give in return for his soul?" (Matt. 16:24–26). "The cross is laid on every Christian," writes the German pastor-theologian Dietrich Bonhoeffer. "It is that dying . . . which is . . . his encounter with Christ. As we embark upon discipleship we surrender ourselves to Christ in union with his death—we give over our lives to death. . . . The cross is not the terrible end to an otherwise godfearing and happy life, but it meets us at the beginning of our communion with Christ. When Christ calls a man, he bids him come and die."[7]

Bonhoeffer's exposition of Jesus' call is clear: the cross we are called to bear is not terrible, but is the beginning of "communion with Christ." Make no mistake: our path ahead as Christians in America—if we choose to follow Jesus—will involve a kind of death. Our allegiance must be wholly to him; as he put it, "No one can serve two masters" (Matt. 6:24). But this kind of death will certainly lead us to life. In another passage about the Christian life, Jesus uses the metaphor of a gate one must pass through: "Enter by the narrow gate. For the gate is wide and the way is easy that leads to destruction, and those who enter by it are many. For the gate is narrow and the way is hard that leads to life, and those who find it are few" (Matt. 7:13–14).

7. Bonhoeffer, *The Cost of Discipleship*, 89.

Dying to What?

What is the cross we will bear? What must we die to? Each chapter before this one outlined the move we must make: from growth to pace, isolation to connection, fame to obscurity, power to vulnerability, wealth to generosity. The New Testament uses the verb "crucify" to speak of how we will put addictions like these to death. It will be painful and slow, but its end is death (Gal. 5:24). Sin works this way: we either put it to death or it puts us to death. We must kill sin before it kills us.[8]

Now comes the final invitation: dying. In the words of Jesus, we must "lay our lives down for our friends" because "greater love has no one than this" (John 15:13). We follow and worship a God who valued his creation (us) over his own status as the Almighty (Phil. 2:6–11). What makes us think we could know God in any significant way while holding our precious little life so close? The apostle Paul prayed boldly that he "may know [Jesus] and the power of his resurrection, and may share his sufferings, becoming like him in his death" (Phil. 3:10).

But we do not die to the pursuit of wealth and growth to be lifeless. We lay down our lives "in Christ," which means we will also be raised (Eph. 2:6; Col. 2:12). We die to greed to live a generous life. We crucify the passion for growth in

8. Tim Keller tweeted this once (https://twitter.com/timkellernyc/status/85 8750314412945409). I couldn't find it published in his books anywhere, but the idea is in his writings. It's not even his idea; John Owen seems to be the Protestant originator of such a concept: "Let no man think to kill sin with few, easy, or gentle strokes. He who hath once smitten a serpent, if he follow not on his blow until it be slain, may repent that ever he began the quarrel. And so he who undertakes to deal with sin, and pursues it not constantly to the death." Quotes like this can be found at a website dedicated to his work: http://johnowen.org /quotes/.

order to live a life of pace. We destroy our lust of power in order to build a life of vulnerability and connection with others.

The entire New Testament invites us into a remarkable, full, satisfying, peaceful, joyous life of abundance, but it comes at a cost. We cannot live the American Story and the biblical one simultaneously. We cannot pursue the American Dream and God's Dream. The two kingdoms are in opposition to one another. Our allegiance must be sworn, and by siding with our King, we are surrendering our life.

This surrender comes with many implications. We will not own the kind of homes we dream of, because we have one awaiting us in heaven. We will not build up massive amounts of wealth in a diversified portfolio reaching global markets all earning us a kind of profit, because we have a different treasure to pursue. We will not reach for power and control in our companies, churches, and organizations, because we know any power we hold is under the Almighty, leading us to value truth more than authority.

Living to What?

On the other side of this death is a resurrection. There is a kind of life out there filled with more security and joy that many who have gone before us have tasted. Jesus Christ himself placed joy as the motivating center of his message of the kingdom of God. "These things I have spoken to you, that my joy may be in you, and that your joy may be full" (John 15:11). Life with him, pursuing the things spoken about in this book, can be compared to a "treasure hidden in a field, which a man found and covered up. Then *in his joy* he goes and sells all that he has and buys that field" (Matt. 13:44, emphasis mine). It's like finding a treasure. Yes, you sell all you have, but you do it in joy because you know there's nothing more valuable than living a life with such strength and integrity.

The people I know who have pursued such a life—one marked by vulnerability and generosity and all the rest— have never looked back. Once you plunge into this life of abandon, the life found only in death, there is no return. Because you have died to the former life and been raised in the new one, you will not be transported back. You will find true life in obscurity, in pace, in connection, and you will remain there like a person who has found a treasure. To borrow another metaphor from Jesus, once your life is hidden in him like yeast in bread, the only thing left to do is to watch it rise (Matt. 13:33). This is the "abundant life" of which Jesus speaks (John 10:10). It is that good.

What It Takes to Get There

The only thing left is to take Jesus at his word, believing that he really means what he says. This is called "faith" or "trust." To take up a full life with Jesus, we must place our faith in him. Faith is not intellectually agreeing with Christianity or nodding our heads as the Bible is read. Faith looks like giving your money away because you take God at his word: "It is more blessed to give than to receive" (Acts 20:35). Because you trust Jesus' way is right, you will actually start giving, trusting it's better than receiving. When Jesus says true life is found in service to others, you will serve others and "value others above yourselves" (Phil. 2:3 NIV). You will do this not because you have to but because you believe God.

Faith is not "believing in God" but "believing God."[9] Read those two statements side by side again—the difference is enormous. Billions of people believe in God, and the Bible says even the demons do (James 2:19), but Christians go further than this: they believe God. When God says something, they say "Amen!" Faith is "the assurance of things hoped for, the conviction of things not seen" (Heb. 11:1). We hear God's word on our lives: to pursue a life of obscurity and pace in a world of growth and fame, to live with vulnerability instead of the pursuit of power, and we say "Amen!" even though we cannot fully see the results. We die *believing God* will show us life.

Faith in the Cross

How can we possibly believe God? Most Americans struggle with believing that God exists, but even more do not believe him. How can we be sure? How can we have the "assurance" of that which we do not see? How can we have faith?

In God's great grace, he has given us the cross. This is where Jesus' earthly life ended, but where the entire Christian movement began. It is where he lost his life and we gained ours. In the cross, we get a vision for how we can believe God.

The cross is where we see the power of God. We see a man, who was also God, dying a death he did not deserve. On the cross, Jesus held the weight of every sin, every piece of our greedy, power-hungry, selfish, and prideful desires. He died a physical death, but with impossible spiritual implications. He died alone, with some of his closest compatriots denying

9. Rodney Anderson, quoted in Stanley, *Deep and Wide*, 95.

they ever knew him. He cried out on that cross, "My God, my God, why have you forsaken me?" (Matt. 27:46; Mark 15:34). He was utterly abandoned in death, and his body was laid in the grave.

But the Christian gospel is called "good news" because Jesus' story did not end there; his life did not end in death—he rose from the dead. In his resurrection, all Christians everywhere have hope and access to trusting God, to not just believing in him but actually believing him. If God raised Jesus from the grave, we too will be raised. Death is no longer "inevitable." We can, like Jesus, lose everything on earth and still remain wealthy. Our names can be known only by our family and no one else and we can still live satisfied because our name is known by God. We come to the cross laying aside any preconceived notion that we can "do it alone," because we realize what Christ has done on our behalf. There is nothing to achieve after meeting Jesus. He's done it all. And our life is hidden in his death, obscurely beautiful.

Our reading of the historical reality of the cross gives us no reason not to take God at his word, to believe him. Now, because of Jesus, we have every reason to believe God brings dead things to life. Our life of rejecting the American Story of More can be embraced with no fear added. Jesus has won; victory is his—we know which story ultimately prevails. We do not need to look any further than the cross to live a life of true faith, in America or any nation. As we face the temptations of greed, power, and growth, we see Jesus: the obscure, poor rabbi from the Middle East who laid his life down for others, dying, only to be raised. Finally and fully, this is where the story ends: not in death, but in life after death; not in hanging on a cross, crucified, but in resurrection.

There is an old prayer written by the German-American theologian and public intellectual Reinhold Niebuhr used in countless recovery and sobriety groups across the world. It's typically called "The Serenity Prayer," and is, in my opinion, one of the best written prayers we have (yes, including the ancients). In it, there's a line asking God that we might learn to be "reasonably happy in this life and supremely happy with him forever in the next." This is what faith is: believing God can grant us true serenity, even within the chaos of America.

Among the Ruins

We wouldn't recognize *that* love. It might even look like hate.
It would be enough to scare us—God's love. It set fire to a
bush in the desert, didn't it, and smashed open graves and
set the dead walking in the dark. Oh, a man like me would
run a mile to get away if he felt that love around.

GRAHAM GREENE, *The Power and the Glory*

Life, our actual existence, is not included in what is now
presented as the heart of the Christian message, or it is
included only marginally. This is where we find ourselves
today. . . . Transformation of life and character is no part of
the [current] redemptive message.

DALLAS WILLARD, *The Divine Conspiracy*

In the opening of her memoir about preaching, the Episcopalian pastor Barbara Brown Taylor writes about a walk she took among the ruins of ancient churches in the

Kachkar Mountains of northeastern Turkey. There, over a thousand years ago, the largest collection of Christians once worshiped in spectacular structures. The church flourished in this part of Turkey for about two hundred years, and then it was all gone. Centuries later, Taylor walked there, reflecting on the parallels between her age and theirs: "It is one thing to talk about the post-Christian era and quite another to walk around inside it."[1] If such an extravagant kind of Christianity in a wealthy era can come to an end, then what makes us think our great-grandchildren won't one day walk among the ruins we are currently creating?

Through her opening chapter, Taylor realizes just how "disillusioned" she and her fellow Americans have become in regard to modern Christianity. From the era of televangelism to our current moment of political polarization inside and outside the church, where "true believers" tout their Scriptures as evidence they're more saved than the others, all seems lost. Liberal or conservative, both sides sound the same to me. I can't help but join in Taylor's "disillusionment" with the Christian faith sometimes, especially when you throw in the word "evangelical." I know many of my generation feel similarly. This is what it means to live in a "post-Christian" society.

"These are grim times," writes Taylor, "in which the God of our fondest dreams is nowhere to be found." I, too, have felt this way, but Taylor refuses to stay in despair. She goes on to write,

> But down in the darkness below those dreams—in the place where all our notions about God have come to naught—there is still reason to hope, because disillusionment is not

1. Taylor, *A Preaching Life*, 4.

so bad. Disillusionment is the loss of illusion—about ourselves, about the world, about God—and while it is almost
always painful, it is not a bad thing to lose the lies we have
mistaken for the truth. Disillusioned, we come to understand
that God does not conform to our expectations. We glimpse
our own relative size in the universe and see that no human
being can say who God should be or how God should act.
We review our requirements of God and recognize them as
our own fictions, our own frail shelters against the vast night
sky. Disillusioned, we find out what is not true and are set
free to seek what is—if we dare.[2]

As you have read this book, you may have felt like Taylor,
walking among the ruins of a society so far from the Christian message that the only end for us is demise. But this is
not the Christian habit of mind. I ended the previous chapter
by talking about faith, and now we need to talk about hope.

Christian hope begins with disillusionment. It starts with
an understanding of our despair without God and moves us
to trust him alone for everything. Hope is the sure expectation that God will do what he says he will do. Hope is the
final and full deep breath of faith, before we plunge into the
unknown. Hope knows that the terrain ahead is strange, for-
eign, and rocky, but that the destination is set. Hope becomes
the Christian's habit of mind when walking among the ruins.

Hope in a Pile of Filth

I, too, had my own walk among the ruins many years ago as
a young pastor. My wife and I led a team of thirty-five high

2. Taylor, *A Preaching Life*, 8.

school students to Managua, Nicaragua, serving alongside local church leaders who had dedicated their lives to rescuing and restoring women out of sex trafficking. Nicaragua is the second poorest nation in the Western hemisphere, and the country has suffered from political corruption alongside natural disasters and economic instability.

On the outskirts of the capital city lies a dump, a wasteland. All of the trash of the city's nearly two million people can be found burning in this heap. "Heap" is the wrong word. It is a city of trash, a pile of filth, disease, poverty, and abuse.

Nearly two hundred families live inside the dump, which is called "La Chureca" by Nicaraguans. These two hundred families total almost one thousand people who call La Chureca their home. The city dump is home to men, women, and children—it is "going home" for hundreds and a place of business for many.

Garbage truck drivers visit La Chureca every day to drop off more trash, and the people of the dump sift through the new garbage all day, mining for something to sell or offer a neighbor as capital. When you enter La Chureca, this is what you see: trash piled four stories high, burning and steaming as people walk through with bags. They are collecting garbage.

The people of La Chureca collect trash and barter and trade for it. Some sell plastic and others collect glass to offer neighbors for a small price or a sexual act. There exists within La Chureca a micro-economy that seems to trap people there for generations.

Already overwhelming, the nightmare gets worse. As the truck drivers come into the dump, the women living in La

Chureca have (many times) been commanded by their fathers to prostitute themselves to the truck drivers for first dibs on the new trash. The girls are abused and often raped, as their fathers would beat them if they did not submit to prostitution. The whole situation seems absurd and horrific, and yet this is their "normal," their way of life.

I toured La Chureca with our students when I was a youth pastor, and I truly believe we saw a picture of hell on earth. I have seen horrific slums and neighborhoods of poverty all around the world, but I have never seen a situation so hopeless as La Chureca.

Jesus' word for hell was a proper noun, *Gehenna*. This is a Greek term that is derived from the Hebrew "Valley of Hinnom," which was as close to La Chureca as it comes: a valley on the outskirts of town where trash was brought to be burned. Dogs and the poor would roam the land in hopes of scraps they could use for food or shelter. The difference was that the Valley of Hinnom was chaotic and La Chureca is ordered. What is so surprising and devastating and disgusting and paralyzing is that there are two hundred families living in this hell.

After my visit to La Chureca, I was overwhelmed to say the least. I sat down with our translator, Mario, and began processing with him:

"I have never seen anything like that, Mario. I thought, before I came here, that I had seen poverty, but I have never seen poverty with such hopelessness, such a lack of choice on the part of the people, such wickedness."

What Mario said to me forever changed my life. "You have never seen it so plainly, you mean," he said.

"I guess. Wait—what do you mean?"

He sat back and spoke up. "In America, you may not be living in such a physical hell, but your experience would tell you that La Chureca is exactly the American situation. It's the same thing, just newer garbage."

He was right.

In America, we rely on trash as our way of life, as our purpose for living. Everything you own right now will be in a dumpster in 150 years. You're just getting it sooner, before it rots in a dump. And your job will be radically reinvented and your industry will totally change in less time. We are sifting through the garbage of this world, our materials, and calling it good for us, a way for us to "make a living." We look to our iPhones, our girlfriends, our husbands, our houses, our cars, our jobs, our own selves, our celebrities, our knowledge, our job descriptions, our accomplishments, our profiles, and our portfolios, and we come up empty and disease ridden. We are not literally sifting through trash, but metaphorically we have placed ourselves in La Chureca and called it "life." The things we love and buy and get tired of just haven't become garbage yet. But they will.

The truth is that the trash used by the people in La Chureca was once good and new. It was once beautiful. It is much like the world, or like us. The world (including us) was made by God, who called it all "good," but in rebelling from him and turning from him, much of the world and much of our lives have rotted before our eyes.

We set ourselves up and say, "This is just the way life is," and we instruct our children to make friends with those who are just adding piles of trash to the heaps every day. We tell them not just to spend time with them, but to commune with them and give ourselves to them. We end up settling for the ruins of the world because our fathers and mothers before us told us that this is "just the way life is." We're not that different from La Chureca.

For the average person, we are a society as destitute as the dump city, but for the Christian, we walk among the ruins disillusioned but also grateful. We realize God hasn't met our expectations—that money, growth, and success would equal happiness and his blessing—but we also realize our expectations were wrong. And right there, at the moment of our disillusionment, we see what some of our brothers and sisters saw in La Chureca: hope.

What Hope Does

Over a decade ago, a local Nicaraguan woman named Gloria began spending time in La Chureca. She volunteered at the school in the middle of the dump and began to meet these young girls and hear about their lives. She saw the way it was and grew disgusted. She saw the way La Chureca has always worked and said, "This is not the way it should be."

So Gloria and her husband, Wilbert, began to talk about what it would look like to rescue these girls, who had no idea of the life that waited for them outside of the dump. Gloria and Wilbert envisioned a house of over forty girls that was far from the dump and in the lush lands of Nicaragua. A paradise with soft beds, caring mothers, and fresh food. A community of houses that had strong foundations and solid ceilings where you could run and play and learn and find safety and refuge. They saw in their minds the way it should be: not a village of trash and garbage, but a village of hope.

Gloria and Wilbert started this house in 2008, and in July of that year the first sixteen girls were welcomed into the Villa Esperanza (in English, "the Village of Hope"). At the villa they met their new house mothers, a vision of what a mother should be, and they met Wilbert, who runs the whole operation, a vision of what a caring father looks like. They inhabited beautiful homes and bunked together, becoming sisters without having to leave their home country.

A few years in, these rescued girls are slowly being saved. Mamá Gloria and Papá Wilbert, as the girls call them, are their saviors from the dump, and the girls will be the first to tell you this.

When you hear these girls pray, they pray in thanks more than anything else. They realize someone from outside the dump had to save them from the torment of life inside the dump. It not only took someone who was out of the mess, but it took someone courageous enough to go into it.

Our Salvation

It would be wise of us to listen to the stories of these girls rescued from La Chureca. They found their salvation from life *inside* the dump by meeting someone *outside*. The solution was not to be found in their immediate purview. They needed a bigger vision for what "life" really is: they were told about an abundant life to be found beyond the dump. They were offered hope.

Our hope is outside the American Story of More. We cannot find salvation within it. So long as we stay here, we will only barter for newer trash. We need help from the outside.

Perhaps that is how we can view this book. I have worked hard to write out a way to relisten to the call of Jesus Christ, the one who has provided us a life and a hope outside the dump. He alone is our salvation. He plunged into our dump of a world and lived among it all. As he did, he laid his life down in order to provide for us not only a vision, but a pathway out. When we see Jesus, we see our hope: we do not need to live this way any longer.

One day, our descendants will walk among the ruins of American culture. They will dig up our megachurches, uncovering our projectors and sound systems. They will excavate the territories of our malls and business parks, parking lots and superstores. They will discover whatever is left of Apple's headquarters and Amazon's many storage facilities; they will pilfer from Google's data farms. And they will wonder why we gave so much to receive so little. The more introspective of them will be forced to examine their own lives, their own connection to their past of materialism, greed, and addiction to growth.[3]

What We Are Building

What are you participating in right now that will matter in ten thousand years? It's a strange question, I know, and nearly impossible to answer without some kind of theology, but I believe it to be a compelling question nonetheless. Are

---

3. See the TV series *Last Man on Earth* or the movies *Idiocracy* (2006) and *Wall-E* (2008). In a similar thought experiment connected to the church, I once heard Francis Chan say he believes historians will view our era of Christian history as the time of "The Consumer Church," where people of all ages believed they were to receive spiritual help from a place they gave their money to, and when they didn't get what they wanted, they'd leave and go somewhere else.

there any activities we can do in this brief little life that will not burn out for thousands and thousands of years?

With the right theological imagination, much of what I've tried to write about here is the kind of stuff that passes into eternity. I've asked us to remember the pace of the kingdom in the face of America's addiction to growth. This kind of participation in what Jesus called "the kingdom of God" gives us a larger scale in which "growth" sits. It's more agricultural than technological, slower than we think.

We would be wise to remember the importance of the table amidst a world of isolation, the triumph of Jesus' local congregations—his church—in a world alone on devices. Before getting too disillusioned and lost in the ruins, pull back and ask yourself some simple questions: Who is coming to my house this week? When I walk into church on Sunday, who might I greet and encourage?

In our tiny life plans, we can reject any kind of self-promotion and power grabbing that we might think would lead us to success, and instead dedicate ourselves to secret acts of kindness and humility. We can celebrate the work of others before our own work, and look at the world in such a way where we imagine who we can serve instead of who we can use. And of course, we are long overdue to take a wholly different look at our money. For brevity's sake, could I put it like this? *Give what you have to the poor.*

All of this might seem a bit ascetic. Maybe it is. But we must listen again to the call of John the Baptizer to "decrease" in an age of increase. All of our data and experience would say that our pursuit for more has given us less. A commitment to less could, then, give us more than we can imagine.

This *is* the way of "salvation," to lose the world in order to gain a soul. If Jesus Christ himself went this route, why would ours be any different? Dying is what brings life, decreasing is what makes the increase. To pour our lives out for five or fifty-five or eighty-five years is what ends up strangely extending them for thousands. Committing our small, short lives to loving the Eternal One provides us with a longer life, what Jesus referred to as "eternal life." What we do today *can* matter in ten thousand years if it is connected to that which exists throughout eternity. But so long as we obsess over and hold tightly to our fifty or eighty years, we will lose it.

The Fall of America and the Resurrection of the Gospel

Make no mistake: the American Empire will fall. There is no historical evidence that our position of power and wealth will last beyond the next two hundred years. The message Jesus spoke of was "the good news of the kingdom of God" (Luke 4:43; 8:1; 16:16), that *his* empire would be "everlasting" and eternal, that his rulership would "have no end" and his people would live with him forever. They would be a part of an "unshakable kingdom" whose founder and architect would be God himself. This kingdom would not be like America or Rome or Greece—not the kind of government you can point out and say, "See!"—it will instead be a kingdom "of God," unseen, eternal, and powerful (Pss. 102:27; 145:13; Dan. 4:3; Luke 4:43; 17:20–21; Acts 8:12; Heb. 11:10; 12:28).

When we become Christians, we become citizens of this kingdom and swear our allegiance to a new king, Jesus. We no longer take orders from the dominant culture, from the popular way of life. We take instructions from our King and we live like him and in him. His Holy Spirit empowers us to live the life he has provided for us in the cross. This life is outside of the dump, away from trading trash with each other. We instead dedicate our lives to one another and to God. We live in a kind of freedom away from our addictions and money, and we consecrate ourselves to serve others. Our money is freely given to those who need it, and we only live on what we absolutely need.

This new life in Christ is available for all people everywhere because we need not earn it, only surrender to it. We submit to Christ as he takes us from the kingdom of America and into the kingdom of heaven. No matter who you are or what kind of business you're involved in, whether you are rich or you are poor, if you are American or not, Jesus gives this invitation to "life abundant" (John 10:10).

When Jesus was on earth and nearing the end of his life, the apostle John recorded this interaction between the disciples and their rabbi. Jesus tells them,

> "Let not your hearts be troubled. Believe in God; believe also in me. In my Father's house are many rooms. If it were not so, would I have told you that I go to prepare a place for you? And if I go and prepare a place for you, I will come again and will take you to myself, that where I am you may be also. And you know the way to where I am going." Thomas said to him, "Lord, we do not know where you are going. How can we know the way?" Jesus said to him, "I am the way, and the truth, and the life. No one comes to the Father except through me. If you had known me, you would have known my Father also. From now on you do know him and have seen him." (John 14:1–7)

To follow Jesus is to follow him out of America and into the kingdom of God, from our own weak, man-made houses and into the mansions he has built that await us. This process—called "salvation"—begins with our surrender to him. We abandon the American Story and we embrace Jesus' life, what I have called the biblical counter-narrative. We join *his story*, leading us to what *he has prepared* for us with a destination no American or other human being could engineer.

You may have heard Christians tell you to "ask Jesus into your life," but that is not the gospel found in Scripture. And that's not what I'm suggesting here. As we see even in the passage above, the invitation is not *from us* to Jesus, but *from Jesus* to us. The difference is paramount. Jesus invites us into *his life*, which looks so impossibly different from ours in the West that we may fail to see it for years. What I have tried to do in this book is what I have tried to do in my life by God's mercy and help: provide a vision of the life of Jesus, how good and true it is, and how accessible he has made it to anyone.

Acknowledgments

My wife, Allison, is the strongest person I know. She remains the foundational support for my entire life of family, ministry, writing, and everything else. She does this while also excelling in her own career as a pediatric anesthesiologist, currently in the madness of residency. Ali, I love you and thank you for your constant, steady support and for showing me what a humble heart before God looks like.

This book would not have been possible without the early, eager support of my agent, Blair Jacobson, of D. C. Jacobson Literary Agency. Thank you to Blair, Don, Marty, and the whole team. Thank you to Baker Publishing Group, especially Brian Thomasson, who demonstrated an understanding of this project from the first time he read it.

I am also grateful for early readers of this book, all of whom gave enormously important feedback. Some, but not all, of those people include Ali Nye, Blair Jacobson, Nicci Jordan Hubert, Jay Kim, Jon Furman, Jordan Chesbrough, Vickie Cozad, John Finnerty, Luke Walker, and my dog, Zo, who withstood my reading aloud while she was trying to nap.

Thank you to our church family, Awakening Church in the Silicon Valley, and more specifically to Ryan Ingram, my boss and lead pastor. Joining this family has been the greatest gift of this year, and your support of my writing means the world to me. Church family, I love serving as one of your pastors.

This book's genesis came from my season of ministry with San Francisco City Impact, where my time on staff with the organization was filled with many essential lessons from the community we served together. In many ways, this one's for the Tenderloin.

I am also grateful to St. Patrick's University and Seminary in Menlo Park, California, for allowing me—and literally anyone—to use their remarkable theological library. Not only do they have every book you could possibly imagine, but their space is quiet and beautiful, and you do not need to spend four dollars on a coffee to stay there for hours.

Major thanks to my family, Mom and Thomas, and the Duggers, who constantly support Ali and me in our crazy life and who offer their homes as respite for reflection and writing when we visit Oregon. Thanks to my brother, Scott, who had a sign above his desk when he was in high school that read WRITE EVERY DAY. I still take that advice and am constantly inspired by your writing. And to Sara and Scott Howes: it's great that the people I most admire are also related to me.

This book is dedicated to my grandfather and grandmother, Gary and Norma Poppinga, who gave me a picture at an early age of the abundant life in Jesus. They were never wealthy, but they have led a tremendously rich life. We lost Grandpa this year, and it reminded me all the more how fortunate we all were to have him as an example of so much of what this book is about. I'm grateful God gave me grandparents like both of you, and I'm convinced my life is what it is because of your daily prayers.

Bibliography

AARP The Magazine. "Loneliness among Older Adults: A National Survey of Adults 45+." *AARP The Magazine,* September 2010. https:// assets.aarp.org/rgcenter/general/loneliness_2010.pdf.

Alcorn, Randy. *Happiness: God's Invitation to Delight, Celebration, and Joy.* Carol Stream, IL: Tyndale, 2015.

————. *Money, Possessions, and Eternity.* Rev. ed. Carol Stream, IL: Tyndale, 2003.

American Foundation for Suicide Prevention. "Suicide Statistics." Accessed September 4, 2018. https://afsp.org/about-suicide/suicide-statistics/.

Associated Press. "Here's How Trump and Clinton Each Say They Would Ignite Economic Growth." *Fortune,* October 2016. http://fortune.com /2016/10/25/trump-clinton-economic-policy-proposals-growth/.

Barth, Karl. *The Epistle to the Romans.* London: Oxford University Press, 1968.

Bell, Rob. *Love Wins: A Book about Heaven, Hell, and the Fate of Every Person Who Ever Lived.* San Francisco: HarperOne, 2012.

Blomberg, Craig L. *Neither Poverty nor Riches: A Biblical Theology of Possessions.* Downers Grove, IL: InterVarsity, 1999.

Bonhoeffer, Dietrich. *The Cost of Discipleship.* New York: Touchstone, 1995.

Brooks, David. "The Benedict Option." *New York Times,* March 14, 2017. https://www.nytimes.com/2017/03/14/opinion/the-benedict -option.html.

———. "The Power of a Dinner Table." *New York Times*, October 18, 2016. https://www.nytimes.com/2016/10/18/opinion/the-power-of-a-dinner-table.html.

Brown, Brené. *Daring Greatly: How the Courage to Be Vulnerable Transforms the Way We Live, Love, Parent, and Lead*. New York: Avery, 2012.

Brueggemann, Walter. *The Land: Place as Gift, Promise, and Challenge in Biblical Faith*. Minneapolis: Fortress Press, 2002.

Bush, George W. "At O'Hare, President Says 'Get On Board.'" Remarks given on September 27, 2001. https://georgewbush-whitehouse.archives.gov/news/releases/2001/09/20010927-1.html.

Campbell, Alexia Fernández. "Why Are Americans Less Charitable Than They Used to Be?" *The Atlantic*, December 2016. https://www.the atlantic.com/business/archive/2016/12/americans-donate-less-to-charity/511397/.

Centers for Disease Control and Prevention. "Depression." FastStats. Accessed September 4, 2018. https://www.cdc.gov/nchs/fastats/de pression.htm.

C.K., Louis. "Louis C.K. Responds to Accusations: 'These Stories Are True.'" *New York Times*, November 10, 2017. https://www.nytimes .com/2017/11/10/arts/television/louis-ck-statement.html.

Collins, Sam P. K. "Americans Are More Depressed Than They've Been in Decades." *Think Progress*, October 2, 2014. https://thinkprogress .org/americans-are-more-depressed-than-theyve-been-in-decades-49 66c49e9faa#.minric9el.

Crouch, Andy. *Playing God*. Downers Grove, IL: InterVarsity, 2013.

———. "Stop Engaging 'The Culture,' Because It Doesn't Exist." *Christianity Today*, June 23, 2016. http://www.christianitytoday.com/ct/2016 /julaug/theculture-doesnt-exist.html?start=2.

Curtin, Sally C., Margaret Warner, and Holly Hedegaard. "Increase in Suicide in the United States, 1999–2014." NCHS data brief, no. 241, April 2016. Hyattsville, MD: National Center for Health Statistics. https://www.cdc.gov/nchs/products/databriefs/db241.htm.

Dargis, Manohla. "Climbing Out of the Gutter with a 5-Year-Old in Tow." *New York Times*, December 15, 2006. http://www.nytimes.com /2006/12/15/movies/15happ.html.

Delbanco, Andrew. *College: What It Was, Is, and Should Be*. Princeton, NJ: Princeton University Press, 2012.

DeLillo, Don. *White Noise*. New York: Penguin, 1986.

Dreher, Rod. *The Benedict Option: A Strategy for Christians in a Post-Christian Nation*. New York: Sentinel, 2017.

———. "Of Sh*tholes and Second Thoughts." *American Conservative*, January 19, 2018. https://www.theamericanconservative.com/dreher /of-shitholes-and-second-thoughts/.

Eggers, Dave. *What Is the What?* New York: Vintage, 2006.

El Issa, Erin. "NerdWallet's 2017 American Household Credit Card Debt Study." NerdWallet. Accessed October 31, 2018. https://www.nerd wallet.com/blog/average-credit-card-debt-household/.

Foster, Dawn. "What Can the UK Learn from How Finland Solved Homelessness?" *Guardian*, March 22, 2017. https://www.theguardian .com/housing-network/2017/mar/22/finland-solved-homelessness-eu -crisis-housing-first.

Francis (pope). *Laudato Si': On Care for Our Common Home*. The Holy See (website). May 24, 2015. http://w2.vatican.va/content/francesco /en/encyclicals/documents/papa-francesco_20150524_enciclica-laud ato-si.html.

Franzen, Jonathan. *Freedom*. New York: Farrar, Straus & Giroux, 2010.

Gao, George. "How Do Americans Stand Out from the Rest of the World?" Pew Research Center, March 12, 2015. http://www.pewre search.org/fact-tank/2015/03/12/how-do-americans-stand-out-from -the-rest-of-the-world/.

Giving USA. "Giving USA 2017: Total Charitable Donations Rise to New High of $390.05 Billion." Press release, June 12, 2017. https://giving usa.org/giving-usa-2017-total-charitable-donations-rise-to-new-high -of-390-05-billion/.

Gladwell, Malcolm. "My Little Hundred Million." *Revisionist History*. Season 1, episode 6. Accessed August 23, 2018. Audio, 42:11. http:// revisionisthistory.com/episodes/06-my-little-hundred-million.

Goggin, Jamin, and Kyle Strobel. *The Way of the Dragon or the Way of the Lamb: Searching for Jesus' Path of Power in a Church That Has Abandoned It*. Nashville: Thomas Nelson, 2017.

Harari, Yuval Noah. *Homo Deus: A Brief History of Tomorrow*. London: Vintage, 2017.

Hari, Johann. *Chasing the Scream*. New York: Bloomsbury, 2016.

——. "Everything You Think You Know about Addiction Is Wrong." TED Talk. https://www.ted.com/talks/johann_hari_everything_you_think_you_know_about_addiction_is_wrong.

Hefner, Chris. "8 Observations of a Revitalized Church." *LifeWay Pastors* (blog), October 9, 2014. https://www.lifeway.com/pastors/2014/10/09/8-observations-about-a-revitalized-church/.

Hellerman, Joseph H. *When the Church Was a Family*. Nashville: B&H Academic, 2009.

Holt-Lunstad, J., T. B. Smith, and J. B. Layton. "Social Relationships and Mortality Risk: A Meta-analytic Review." *PLOS Medicine* 7, no. 7 (2010): e1000316. https://doi.org/10.1371/journal.pmed.1000316.

Hongo, Jun. "Homelessness in Tokyo Hits Record Low." *Japan Real Time* (blog). *Wall Street Journal*, October 17, 2014. https://blogs.wsj.com/japanrealtime/2014/10/17/homelessness-in-tokyo-hits-record-low/.

Keller, Timothy. "Dr. Timothy Keller at Reformed Theological Seminary: Lecture 2." YouTube video, 53:40. Posted by ReformedSeminary, November 25, 2014. https://www.youtube.com/watch?v=oHPB0Msasak&t=2456s.

Khullar, Druhv. "How Social Isolation Is Killing Us." *The Upshot* (blog), December 22, 2016. https://www.nytimes.com/2016/12/22/upshot/how-social-isolation-is-killing-us.html.

Klosterman, Chuck. *Eating the Dinosaur*. New York: Scribner, 2009.

Kolbert, Elizabeth. "No Time." *New Yorker*, May 26, 2014. https://www.newyorker.com/magazine/2014/05/26/no-time.

Leasca, Stacey. "Here's the Very Scary Amount of Money Americans Spend On Halloween." *Forbes*, October 30, 2017. https://www.forbes.com/sites/sleasca/2017/10/30/halloween-spending-halloween-candy/#62b50da620a1halloween-candy/#62b50da620a1.

Lee, Kristin. "The Unsettling Truth about What's Hurting Today's Students." *Psychology Today*, January 23, 2018. https://www.psychologytoday.com/us/blog/rethink-your-way-the-good-life/201801/the-unsettling-truth-about-what-s-hurting-today-s.

Leovy, Jill. *Ghettoside: A True Story of Murder in America*. New York: Spiegel & Grau, 2015.

Lewis, C. S. *Miracles*. New York: HarperCollins, 1996.

———. *The Screwtape Letters*. San Francisco: HarperOne, 1996.

———. *Surprised by Joy*. San Diego: Harcourt Brace, 1955.

Lipka, Michael. "Major U.S. Metropolitan Areas Differ in Their Religious Profiles." Pew Research Center, July 29, 2015. http://www.pewresearch .org/fact-tank/2015/07/29/major-u-s-metropolitan-areas-differ-in -their-religious-profiles/.

Live Science Staff. "Half of All Friends Replaced Every 7 Years." https:// www.livescience.com/5466-friends-replaced-7-years.html.

Maron, Marc. "Ta-Nehisi Coates." *WTF with Marc Maron*. Episode 878, January 4, 2018. Audio. http://www.wtfpod.com/podcast/episode -878-ta-nehisi-coates.

Martin, Courtney E. *The New Better Off: Reinventing the American Dream*. Berkeley, CA: Seal Press, 2016.

Martin, Emmie. "Nearly 70% of Americans Consider Themselves Middle-Class—Here's How Many Actually Are." CNBC (website). September 26, 2018. https://www.cnbc.com/2018/09/26/how-many -americans-qualify-as-middle-class.html.

Max, Daniel T. *Every Love Story Is a Ghost Story: A Life of David Foster Wallace*. New York: Viking, 2012.

———. "Rereading David Foster Wallace - The New Yorker Festival - The New Yorker." Panel discussion with Mary Karr, Dana Spiotta, Mark Costello, and Deborah Triesman. YouTube video, 1:30:57. Posted by The New Yorker, July 22, 2014. https://www.youtube.com/watch?v=Jq N52yKI4pg.

McCracken, Brett. "Has 'Authenticity' Trumped Holiness?" *The Gospel Coalition* (website), January 26, 2014. https://www.thegospelcoalition .org/article/has-authenticity-trumped-holiness-2/.

McFague, Sallie. *Speaking in Parables: A Study in Metaphor and Theology*. Minneapolis: Augsburg Fortress, 2000.

McKibben, Bill. *Deep Economy: The Wealth of Communities and the Durable Future*. New York: Times Books, 2007.

———. "The Most Important Number in the World." Annual E. F. Schumacher Lecture, October 2009, Schumacher Center for a New

Economics. http://www.centerforneweconomics.org/publications
/lectures/mckibben/bill/the-most-important-number-in-the-world.

———. "The Pope and the Planet." *The New York Review of Books,*
August 13, 2015. http://www.nybooks.com/articles/2015/08/13/pope
-and-planet/.

Mislinski, Jill. "U.S. Household Incomes: A 50-Year Perspective." *Advisor Perspectives* (website), September 19, 2017. https://www.advisor
perspectives.com/dshort/updates/2016/09/15/u-s-household-incomes
-a-49-year-perspective.

Murray, Andrew. *Absolute Surrender.* Los Angeles: IndoEuropean Publishing, 2011.

Neighmond, Patti. "Overworked Americans Aren't Taking the Vacation
They've Earned." *All Things Considered,* July 12, 2016. http://www
.npr.org/sections/health-shots/2016/07/12/485606970/overworked
-americans-arent-taking-the-vacation-theyve-earned.

Nouwen, Henri. "From Solitude to Community to Ministry." *Leadership
Journal* (Spring 1995). http://www.christianitytoday.com/pastors/1995
/spring/5l280.html.

———. *In the Name of Jesus: Reflections on Christian Leadership.* New
York: Crossroads, 1989.

NPR. "Stretched: Working Parents' Juggling Act." NPR Special Series.
https://www.npr.org/series/496729626/stretched-challenges-facing
-working-parents-in-the-u-s.

Nye, Chris. *Distant God: Why He Feels Far Away . . . and What We Can
Do about It.* Chicago: Moody, 2016.

O'Connor, Flannery. *Everything That Rises Must Converge.* New York:
Farrar, Straus & Giroux, 1965.

Osborne, Larry. "The Myth of Endless Growth." *Larry Osborne Live*
(blog), August 20, 2012. https://larryosbornelive.com/the-myth-of
-endless-growth/.

Outreach. "100 Fastest-Growing Churches in America 2016." http://www
.outreachmagazine.com/outreach-100-fastest-growing-churches-2016
.html (list has subsequently been removed from website).

Outreach. "Outreach 100." Accessed November 5, 2018. https://outreach
magazine.com/outreach-100.html.

Outside in America Team. "Bussed Out: How America Moves Its Homeless." *Guardian*, December 20, 2017. https://www.theguardian.com/us-news/ng-interactive/2017/dec/20/bussed-out-america-moves-homeless-people-country-study.

PBS. "Generation Like." *Frontline*. No date. https://www.pbs.org/wgbh/frontline/film/generation-like/transcript/.

Peterson, Eugene. *Under the Unpredictable Plant: An Exploration in Vocational Holiness*. Grand Rapids: Eerdmans, 1992.

————. *Working the Angles: The Shape of Pastoral Integrity*. Grand Rapids: Eerdmans, 1987.

Pfeffer, Jeffrey. *Power: Why Some People Have It—and Others Don't*. New York: HarperBusiness, 2010.

Piper, John. "For His Sake and Your Joy, Go Low." Sermon delivered December 17, 2011, at Bethlehem Baptist Church. https://www.desiringgod.org/messages/for-his-sake-and-for-your-joy-go-low.

Plantinga, Cornelius, Jr. *Not the Way It's Supposed to Be: A Breviary of Sin*. Grand Rapids: Eerdmans, 1996.

Putnam, Robert D. *Bowling Alone: The Collapse and Revival of American Community*. New York: Simon & Schuster, 2007.

Quinones, Sam. *Dreamland: The True Tale of America's Opiate Epidemic*. New York: Bloomsbury Press, 2016.

Rachleff, Andy. "What 'Disrupt' Really Means." *TechCrunch*, February 16, 2013. https://techcrunch.com/2013/02/16/the-truth-about-disruption.

Radner, Ephraim. *Leviticus*. Brazos Theological Commentary on the Bible. Grand Rapids: Brazos, 2008.

Rainer, Thom. "2014 Update on Largest Churches in the Southern Baptist Convention." *Thom Rainer* (blog), July 12, 2014. http://thomrainer.com/2014/07/2014-update-largest-churches-southern-baptist-convention/.

Remnick, David. "Obama Reckons with a Trump Presidency." *New Yorker*, November 28, 2016. http://www.newyorker.com/magazine/2016/11/28/obama-reckons-with-a-trump-presidency.

Roberts, Robert C. "Self-Perception and Humility: The Importance of an Accurate Self-Image." *The Table*, September 28, 2017. https://cct.biola.edu/growing-humility-accurate-self-perception-can-lead-humility/.

Rolheiser, Ronald. *The Holy Longing: The Search for a Christian Spirituality*. New York: Image, 2014.

Ronson, Jon. *So You've Been Publicly Shamed*. New York: Vintage, 2015.

Rose, Charlie. "David Foster Wallace." March 27, 1997. https://charlie rose.com/videos/23311.

Rosenblat, Josh. "The Wealthier You Get, the Less Social You Are. Here's Why It Matters." *Vox*, May 5, 2016. https://www.vox.com/2016/5/5 /11578994/income-friends-family.

Rosin, Hanna. "The Silicon Valley Suicides." *The Atlantic*, December 2015. https://www.theatlantic.com/magazine/archive/2015/12/the -silicon-valley-suicides/413140/.

Rutledge, Fleming. *The Crucifixion: Understanding the Death of Jesus Christ*. Grand Rapids: Eerdmans, 2016.

Ryzik, Melena, Cara Buckley, and Jodi Kantor. "Louis C.K. Is Accused by 5 Women of Sexual Misconduct." *New York Times*, November 9, 2017. https://www.nytimes.com/2017/11/09/arts/television/louis-ck -sexual-misconduct.html.

Sailhamer, John. *The NIV Compact Bible Commentary*. Grand Rapids: Zondervan, 1994.

Schwartz, Barry. "Tyranny of Choice." *Chronicle of Higher Education*, January 23, 2004. https://www.chronicle.com/article/The-Tyranny -of-Choice/22622.

Sherman, Erik. "America Is the Richest, and Most Unequal, Country." *Fortune*, September 30, 2015. http://fortune.com/2015/09/30/america -wealth-inequality/.

Stanford University. "Stanford Management Company Releases 2016 Results." News, September 28, 2016. http://news.stanford.edu/2016/09 /28/stanford-management-company-releases-2016-results/.

Stanley, Andy. *Deep and Wide: Creating Churches Unchurched People Love to Attend*. Grand Rapids: Zondervan, 2012.

Statista. "Average Daily Consumer Spending in the U.S. from July 2016 to July 2017 (in U.S. Dollars)." https://www.statista.com/statistics/20 5241/us-self-reported-consumer-spending-by-month/.

Stokes, Trevor. "You Gotta Have Friends? Most Have Just 2 True Pals." *NBC News*, November 2, 2015. https://www.nbcnews.com/health

/health-news/you-gotta-have-friends-most-have-just-2-true-pals-f1 C6436540.

Stott, John. *The Cross of Christ*. Downers Grove, IL: InterVarsity, 2006.

Student Loan Hero. "A Look at the Shocking Student Loan Debt Statistics for 2018." Updated May 1, 2018. https://studentloanhero.com/student -loan-debt-statistics/.

Tavernise, Sabrina. "U.S. Suicide Rate Surges to a 30-Year High." *New York Times*, April 22, 2016. https://www.nytimes.com/2016/04/22 /health/us-suicide-rate-surges-to-a-30-year-high.html?_r=0.

Taylor, Barbara Brown. *A Preaching Life*. Cambridge, MA: Cowley Pub- lications, 1993.

Tippett, Krista. "Richard Rodriguez: The Fabric of Our Identity." *On Being*, September 18, 2014. Audio, 51:00. https://onbeing.org/programs /richard-rodriguez-the-fabric-of-our-identity/.

Tumblr. "A New Policy against Self-Harm Blogs." *Tumblr Staff* (blog), February 23, 2012. https://staff.tumblr.com/post/18132624829/self -harm-blogs.

Van Cleave, Kris. "2016 May Go Down as One of the Worst Years for Drunk-Driving Deaths." *CBS News*, December 26, 2016. http://www .cbsnews.com/news/2016-may-go-down-as-one-of-the-worst-years -for-drunk-driving-deaths/.

Wallace, David Foster. *Infinite Jest*. New York: Back Bay Books, 2006.

Whitaker, Robert. *Anatomy of an Epidemic: Magic Bullets, Psychiatric Drugs, and the Astonishing Rise of Mental Illness in America*. New York: Broadway Paperbacks, 2010.

White, Charles Edward. "Four Lessons on Money: From One of the World's Richest Preachers." *Christian History* 19 (Summer 1998): 24. https:// www.christianitytoday.com/history/issues/issue-19/four-lessons-on -money.html.

Wikipedia. "List of Countries by Homeless Population." Accessed August 31, 2018. https://en.wikipedia.org/wiki/List_of_countries_by_home less_population.

Willard, Dallas. *The Divine Conspiracy: Rediscovering Our Hidden Life in God*. San Francisco: HarperOne, 1998.

Willimon, William H. *Pastor: The Theology and Practice of Ordained Ministry*. Nashville: Abingdon, 2002.

Wilson, Jared C. *The Prodigal Church*. Wheaton: Crossway, 2015.

Wines, Michael. "A Sharp Spike in Honeybee Deaths Deepens a Worrisome Trend." *New York Times*, May 13, 2015. https://www.nytimes.com/2015/05/14/us/honeybees-mysterious-die-off-appears-to-worsen.html.

Wolfe, Tom. "Tom Wolfe on How to Write New Journalism." Interview by James Kaplan. *Rolling Stone*, November 5, 1987. https://www.rollingstone.com/music/music-features/tom-wolfe-on-how-to-write-new-journalism-90742/.

Wright, Bradley R. E. *Christians Are Hate-Filled Hypocrites . . . and Other Lies You've Been Told*. Minneapolis: Bethany House, 2010.

Yeginsu, Ceylan. "U.K. Appoints a Minister for Loneliness." *New York Times*, January 17, 2018. https://www.nytimes.com/2018/01/17/world/europe/uk-britain-loneliness.html.

Yonack, Lyn. "Sexual Assault Is about Power: How #MeToo Campaign Is Restoring Power to Victims." *Psychology Today*, November 14, 2017. https://www.psychologytoday.com/blog/psychoanalysis-unplugged/201711/sexual-assault-is-about-power.

Chris Nye is a pastor and writer living in California's Bay Area with his wife, Allison. He is most recently the author of *Distant God: Why He Feels Far Away . . . and What We Can Do about It*, and his writing has appeared in the *Washington Post, Christianity Today, RELEVANT Magazine,* and various other publications. Chris currently serves as a pastor for leadership development and teaching at Awakening Church, a faith community reaching the Silicon Valley. He also travels throughout the United States speaking at churches, universities, and retreats. Visit www.chrisnye.co for more.

GET CONNECTED WITH

CHRISNYE

www.chrisnye.co

f pastor**chris**nye

y **chris**nye

o **chris**nye